Tribal Hero
SHIBU SOREN

Tribal Hero
SHIBU SOREN

Anuj Kumar Sinha

PRABHAT PRAKASHAN

Published by
PRABHAT PRAKASHAN PVT. LTD.
4/19 Asaf Ali Road,
New Delhi-110 002 (INDIA)
e-mail: prabhatbooks@gmail.com

ISBN 978-93-90366-52-1
TRIBAL HERO SHIBU SOREN
by Shri Anuj Kumar Sinha

Edition
First, 2023

Price
₹ 700.00 (Rupees Seven Hundred Rupees only)

Printed at
R-Tech Offset Printers, Delhi

My Thoughts

This book, 'Dishom Guru : Shibu Soren' is a story of the life of Shibu Soren, the greatest Adivasi leader of the Jharkhand Movement. There is a specific purpose of writing this book - to make the entire country and the world aware of Shibu Soren's struggles and contribution to the heritage of Jharkhand that the current generation is unaware of.

'Jharkhand Aandolan Ka Dastavej : Shoshan, Sangharsh Aur Shahadat' was my first book. This was a story about the people who participated in the Jharkhand Movement and either lost their lives or got severely injured. It was intended to make the country aware of those who attained martyrdom or made a significant contribution for the creation of Jharkhand state. The book was aimed to help them get a place in history and ensure that future generations remember them with respect. The book was also written with the aim of bringing to light all the contributions Shibu Soren made in the elimination of the money-lending system, creation of a separate Jharkhand state and the initiation of social reform movements among the Adivasis. There is no doubt that Shibu Soren, popularly addressed by some as 'Guruji' and by others as 'Dishom Guru', made the longest and the most relentless struggle for a separate Jharkhand state. No other leader has received the title of 'Dishom Guru'. This is a great honour. Shibu Soren's movement, extending over a period of 40 years for a separate Jharkhand state, is not a petty affair. During that period, he spent most of his time in villages and Parasnath hills. The fight for a separate state was initiated only later; before that, he launched movement for releasing the Adivasis from the clutches of moneylenders and liberating the Adivasi society from prevailing social evils. This is the movement that resulted in elimination of the money-lending system in Jharkhand. He enabled the Adivasis to lead a respectable life. There was a time when moneylenders and pawnbrokers used to usurp the lands of the Adivasis either by force or by deceit; he restored possession of those lands to the Adivasis. The country is still not aware of

Shibu Soren's struggle that achieved the same. The current generation does not know how Shibu Soren kept his movement going while spending his days in forests and hills and how he dedicated his entire youth for the movement. They only know that Shibu Soren had launched the agitation for a separate Jharkhand state and also had been jailed like many other leaders; and that he was the chief minister of Jharkhand. He was even accused of many serious charges and had spent days in jails in cases ranging from murder to bribery. Today's generation has only this kind of incomplete information about Shibu Soren. People do not have the information about the real Shibu Soren - the information that establishes Shibu Soren as the hero of the Adivasi movement. The purpose of writing this book is to introduce to the country the real Shibu Soren i.e., Shibu Soren, the hero.

I have been in contact with Shibu Soren for a long time. I am in journalism for over 35 years and my contact with him also extends to almost the same period. I have also been associated with the Jharkhand Movement and agitators. I have been a part of the same. Hence, it's my responsibility to reveal to the country the facets of his, I mean Guruji's life, that people are not aware of; this only would be justice to him. Despite knowing everything, if I don't do this, I would have regret for my entire life for not being able to bring to light the finer aspects of the character of a sincere Adivasi leader and a person with such a fighting spirit. The book also contains some of my personal experiences (my moments with him) that would help people to appreciate the real Shibu Soren. Guruji has often been blamed for promoting nepotism; but reading this book would reveal how Guruji had replaced his son Durga Soren with a common worker Sunil Mahto as a candidate for Jamshedpur, how he exhibited great patience and managed to calm the domicile movement that was burning Jharkhand and how he raised a boy from a poor family on his own expense and made him a teacher. Such examples are there in abundance. Of course, some of his shortcomings are also discussed in this book.

This book is not the result of only six months or one year of efforts. I have worked on this for almost twenty years. During those twenty years, I even met some of the old associates of Shibu Soren's movement and tried to collect all the information. I myself have been witness to many of those events. Thus, these details are authentic. Except for a few, almost all of those friends and associates of Shibu Soren have left for their heavenly abode. The individuals from whom I could collect all these details were, together with Shibu Soren, part of his social campaigns and the Jharkhand Movement. Be it Dhan Singh Munda, Jhagru Pandit, Digambar Marandi or Rajendra Tiwari - they all have been old associates of Shibu Soren in his movement. Every attempt has been made in this book to present the events in a way such that they appear very true to life. Accordingly, most of the time, details have been narrated in the words of those fellow workers of Guruji or the people linked to the events. Right from Shibu Soren's movement to his political life, his family, his character and his lifestyle - everything has been covered in this book. It's not easy to understand this great Adivasi leader - the leader who even today, enjoys the popularity that prompts thousands of Adivasi people to travel barefoot, with food packed in their clothes, for 50-60 km to listen to him, whose one call used to make thousands of Adivasi people assemble in no time armed with their conventional weapons and who was able to avoid police bullets on the strength of the protective shield created by the people. The book reveals how Shibu Soren is always ready to help a common man.

Most of the people are not aware that Guruji neither drinks nor takes non-vegetarian food. He has fought against hariya drinking since the beginning. He even used to beat people who indulged in drinking. He used to run a parallel government in Tundi and teach farming to the Adivasis; he used to run a night school for this purpose and train people in animal husbandry. He transformed the lives of thousands of Adivasis with the help of these very endeavours. He had his own model for development. He used to run his 19-point programme. Such a popular leader had to go to jail in Chirudih case, JMM bribery case and the Shashi Nath Jha murder case; he was however acquitted by the court in all the cases. These incidents are described in detail in this book. There are some exclusive materials about his relationship with leaders like Binod Bihari Mahato, A. K. Roy, Nirmal Mahto and Gyan Ranjan. Most of these materials are coming out in the open for the first time. Hence, I hope readers would appreciate them.

IAS officer K. B. Saxena has played an important role in taking Shibu Soren out of the forests and bringing him to the mainstream. The book has detailed accounts of why K. B. Saxena was posted as the DC of Dhanbad and how he changed his mind after meeting Shibu Soren in Palma. His thoughts about Shibu Soren underwent a transformation. Only after this did Shibu Soren surrender. There is detailed discussion on the roles of Police officer B. Kichingya and the then Chief Minister of Bihar Dr. Jagannath Mishra in persuading Guruji, and their opinions about Shibu Soren. Prominent journalist of the country and editor of the magazine 'Dinman' Mr Jawaharlal Kaul had visited Tundi during 1975-76 to personally have a look at the works of Shibu Soren. His views are covered in this book. How was the political career of Shibu Soren, how did he rise to be a parliamentarian, a minister and a chief minister and how did he lose his election while still holding the office of the chief minister - all these are also discussed in detail in this book.

It would not have been possible for me to write this book had Guruji's old friends and associates not extended their help from time to time. It has been my endeavour to trace Guruji's old friends involved in his movement, talk to them and gather as much information as possible. Those old associates had described the events in vivid details making them appear to be happening in front of our eyes. Hence, they were immensely helpful in completing this book. I am grateful to Dhan Singh Munda (since deceased), Jhagru Pandit, Murlidhar, Rajendra Tiwari, Shailendra Mahto, L. K. Jha and L. K. Sahay; they have provided a lot of details. Being Guruji's friend right from the days in Bokaro, Dhan Singh Munda had the opportunity to spend a lot of time with him. He was witness to many of the events; hence, the details he provided are authentic. My friend in Patna,Mithlesh has also made a significant contribution. Interviewing Dr. Jagannath Mishra was not an easy job; its credit goes to Mithlesh only. Dr. Mishra was highly instrumental in persuading Shibu Soren to surrender and later arranging his meeting with Prime Minister Indira Gandhi. Anand, my friend in Dumka, managed to fish out some old photographs, though he had to make a lot of efforts for the same. He is quite enthusiastic. He also provided some interesting information; a lot of thanks to him. Mithlesh Jha from Ranchi, Himanshu from Chandil, Nageshwar from Gomia and Sanjeev from Dhanbad - their contributions also have been noteworthy. Sanjeev's father L. K. Jha (since deceased) used to attend Guruji's programmes during 1975-76. I was able to get some valuable information from him; I am thankful to him. My friend Ajay from Ranchi helped in searching out old newspapers. A number of crucial documents were received from Shailendra Mahto. Some documents received from Veer Bharat Talwar, Dr. H. K. Singh of XISS and Girdhari Ram Gonjhu were also quite helpful. Thanks to all of them. I am thankful to my colleagues Umesh and Manish of 'Prabhat Khabar' for making this book attractive. I am also obliged to my friends who accompanied me in my visits to the places linked to Guruji, to Tundi and some villages located at the foothills of Parasnath. There were many unapproachable locations where people were not willing to come with me. I am hence thankful to all of them who did.

I hope readers appreciate this book as it will be able to enlighten them about Shibu Soren as well as all his former associates whom Guruji had lost during the movement. Thanks again.

-Anuj Kumar Sinha

Ranchi

Contents

Popular Adivasi Leader

The Jharkhand Movement was witness to many great leaders and workers, their struggles and their resolve to march ahead. Eminent names like Jaipal Singh, N. E. Horo, Devendra Manjhi, Bagun Sumbrui, Binod Bihari Mahto, Nirmal Mahto, A. K. Roy and Shibu Soren figure in that list. It may be a matter of debate to decide or determine who actually was the greatest leader of the Jharkhand Movement; however, this may be said without doubt that Shibu Soren has been one of the most popular and resolute leaders of the Movement. This is because Shibu Soren not only fought for a separate Jharkhand state but also ensured its culmination. He also successfully led the social reform movements of the Adivasis. His struggle for social reforms and for elimination of money-lending system puts him in a different league. The Jharkhand Movement had picked up steam under the leadership of Jaipal Singh but lost its momentum later, and it was Guruji i.e., Shibu

Soren only who carried that movement forward on his shoulders to ensure attainment of its goal. It may not be appropriate to compare the two, as their periods of action were entirely different, the circumstances were different, fighting styles were different. However, there was one thing common to both. Both were powerful and popular leaders of their groups and their decisions were always final and acceptable to all. While Jaipal Singh, during the period 1938 to 1963 (before merger), raised the voices of the Adivasis and got them heard in the assembly and the parliament, Shibu Soren fought the decisive battle right from 1967-68 up to 2000 (till creation of Jharkhand state). He took the movement that had germinated in the villages of Jharkhand to the streets of Patna, Kolkata and Delhi and stopped only when a separate Jharkhand state was created on 15 November 2000. The struggle of Shibu Soren never lost steam even while the governments and chief ministers and prime ministers in the state and the centre kept changing in the meanwhile. He kept the movement running, though its intensity did go up and down - sometimes with demonstrations and rallies and at other times with economic blockades and bandhs.

Shibu Soren

Almost every movement had an impact. Hence, if credit for creation of a separate Jharkhand state and elimination of money-lending system has to be attributed to any Adivasi leader, he can be nobody else other than Guruji (Shibu Soren). If only Shibu Soren had not got involved in controversies relating to some cases and, instead of assuming some positions, had retired from politics immediately after creation of separate Jharkhand state, his position in Indian politics would have been immensely high. However, it does not mean that his decision not to retire has undermined his status anyway. His magic was always felt, whether he was in or out of power. He has a unique way to live his life and to speak. No journalist can muster the courage to get an answer from him if he is not willing to respond to a question, but when he is in an open mood, his answers strike a chord and touch the heart of any person listening to him. Here is an example.

When somebody once asked Guruji about his intention of becoming chief minister, he replied very plainly, “If not for becoming chief minister, have I launched this movement for cutting grass?” He is, even today,the most popular leader of the Adivasis across the country. It’s a different matter that Shibu Soren restricted himself to Jharkhand or greater Jharkhand only.

The Adivasis in Jharkhand have been fighting for years for their demands. They have their own problems. Jaipal Singh was their leader only during the initial years (after 1938). After independence, when elections were held for Bihar Assembly in the year 1952, the Jharkhand Party demonstrated its strength and secured the status of the main opposition party by winning 32 seats. Congress sensed their strength and hence, they set up a trap and Jaipal Singh got caught in the same. He merged Jharkhand Party into Congress. The Jharkhand Movement lost its steam after this. Many questions were raised; there were protests also. People even made comments that the movement had been sold out. Jaipal Singh might be having his own justifications for his move to go with Congress. Later, N. E. Horo, Bagun Sumbrui and Devendra Manjhi somehow managed to keep the Jharkhand Movement alive. Had Jaipal Singh not merged Jharkhand Party into Congress, Jharkhand state would have come into existence much earlier. And in that case, Shibu Soren would not have got the opportunity to demonstrate his potential that, in fact, created his identity. It may even be said that one wrong step (merger) of Jaipal Singh laid the path for Shibu Soren and he treaded that very path to bring together all the Adivasis and secure a separate Jharkhand. He created history!

As such, Jaipal Singh also was a popular leader of the Adivasis. He was recognised all across the country. None of his opponents had the courage to interrupt him whenever he spoke in the parliament as a voice of the Adivasis. Congress somehow got his party merged to blunt this very strength of Jaipal Singh. That was a mistake. Shibu Soren did not make any such mistake. He never allowed the identity of Jharkhand Mukti Morcha to get diluted. Though Shibu Soren did get lured to Congress Party's bluffs at many occasions, he managed to recoup himself. He did enter into electoral alliances with Congress but always on his own terms. He never pledged his party. Shibu Soren was always successful in making Congress realise the strength of JMM.

When, during the emergency, some of the top leaders of Congress had intervened and created an atmosphere, by withdrawing the court cases against him, for him to come out of the forests and surrender, there was a fear that Shibu Soren also might get lost in the crowd of Congress, and thus lose his identity. There were also some attempts in this regard. Two prominent leaders - Binod Bihari Mahto and A. K. Roy did get alienated from Shibu Soren because of the alliance between JMM and Congress. They both gradually got alienated from JMM also. The party was close to getting disintegrated. However, Shibu Soren used his prowess to save the party. This happened as Shibu Soren had learnt a lesson from the past. He did not want to repeat the history. He understood how much faith the Adivasis had in him. He was aware that it was Congress who needed him or JMM and not the other way round. Hence, Congress could never prevail over Shibu Soren completely.

With family on his birthday

Shibu Soren is a highly experienced politician. He knew when and how to deal with a party and when to align with somebody. This is the reason that he aligned sometimes with UPA and sometimes with NDA. He knew when to support Lalu Prasad government and when to support Nitish Kumar government in Bihar. He was never subservient to any particular party. He kept on taking decisions as per his own conscience depending on the circumstances. Nobody had the courage to go against his decisions. He has the art of perception of time. The moment Lalu Prasad made the statement that a separate state would be created on his 'dead body', Shibu Soren took no time in severing his relationship with him. He aligned with NDA when he felt that the same would help in creation of separate Jharkhand state. It is a different matter that this kind of attitude did result in loss for him sometimes. Shibu Soren was with the NDA when the bill relating to Jharkhand state was passed in 2000. He was confident that his alignment with NDA would not only help in creation of Jharkhand state but also provide him opportunity to be the first chief minister of the state. With that very thinking, he had supported Nitish Kumar of NDA and not Lalu Prasad for forming the government in Bihar, but once the new Jharkhand state was created, BJP did not hand over the power to him. Even then, Shibu Soren tried his best. He met Prime Minister Atal Bihari Vajpayee, Home Minister Lal Krishna Advani and NDA coordinator George Fernandes to stake his claim. When NDA did not concede, he shifted to UPA. It's a fact that Shibu Soren has always wielded his power. That is the reason that both NDA and UPA have always strived to secure his support. The real reason behind that has been the Adivasi vote bank. Shibu Soren assumed the position of the chief minister of Jharkhand at different times with the support of both NDA and UPA. This reflects his influence in the politics of the state.

Shibu Soren has played a significant role in the fight for a respectable life for the Adivasi community. He is a born fighter. Burning in the fire of revenge after the death of his father, he discontinued his study. He was just 13-14 years old then. He gradually started fighting for his rights. Later, this very temperament took him to initiate fight against the moneylenders. This movement kept on spreading out. The Adivasis were getting ruined by the moneylenders. It reached a point when the Adivasi community got confident that only Shibu Soren could transform their lives. Only he was capable of reclaiming the lands that the moneylenders had usurped from them. And this is what happened. Shibu Soren did not worry for his family alone, he was concerned for the entire Adivasi community and he fought for them. He spent all of his youth in the villages and forests located at the foothills of Parasnath. It's difficult to find another leader in the history of Jharkhand who would have dedicated his entire life for the cause of the Adivasi community. Shibu Soren's movement grew to be so widespread that its reverberations were felt even in Delhi. It was because of this powerful movement, that on the instructions of the then Prime Minister Indira Gandhi, the erstwhile Chief Minister Jagannath Mishra persuaded him and withdrew the cases against him to pave the way for him to join the mainstream. This was by the power of his movement only. He not only got the lands back to the Adivasis, but also taught them farming, reading and writing, and animal husbandry. There are very few such examples in the history of India. It's not that he only organised the 'cut down paddy' movement. When he felt that the Adivasi community would not be able to reap any benefits until they got political rights, he did not refrain from jumping even into politics. He took the movement forward politically by sending himself and his colleagues to the parliament and state assembly. Of course, Shibu Soren ensured during the entire movement that the fights of the farms are carried out in the farms only; they should be aimed only towards those who they were fighting against. There was no dearth of his enemies, thanks to this movement. Even moneylenders had made attempts for his murder on many occasions but some divine power kept protecting him every time. He was once attacked by the moneylenders near Barakar River. He was then riding a motorcycle. He just jumped into the river along with his motorcycle to save himself. The river was in full flow. The moneylenders assumed Shibu Soren to have drowned and left, but he managed to swim for some time and get across the river. By that time, the news of attack on him had already spread to villages. People were surprised to see him alive. This was ascribed to some divine miracle only. From that very day, people started calling him 'Dishom Guru'.

During the course of the movement against moneylenders, his single call or dugdugi used to prompt thousands of Adivasis to gather at one place armed with their weapons; they would corner the moneylenders but there was not a single incident involving any kind of misbehaviour with any woman. This happened because it was Shibu Soren's clear instruction for the agitators not to deviate from their path. On the contrary, instances have come to light where many of the moneylenders, whose lands were taken over, later joined the movement to support Shibu Soren. Shibu Soren also provided all the help on personal level to enable them to start their life afresh. Guruji has always given a lot of importance to personal relations. Even today, when his old companions of the movement, belonging to far off villages in Santhal Pargana, come to see him at his residence in Ranchi, he personally makes sure they are taken care of properly. Not only that, he also personally ensures that everybody has adequate money to cover return fare before they are seen off. This has been his character.

Truly, he is a leader who is able to draw people from far off places to come and listen to him. The meetings many a time run for entire nights and his supporters hang on till the end. He has his own way of contesting elections or conveying his messages. He is able to convert a losing position in his favour. Even his appeal for help of only one handful of rice and one rupee during elections leaves a major impact. If required, he does not even hesitate to make campaign announcements himself by beating drums. While speaking from a podium, he sometimes uses the language that no other Adivasi leader has the courage to use. The Adivasi community has endowed him with the right to admonish or reprimand people from a platform. He sometimes even uses words that if spoken by anybody else would have provoked the ire of listeners. This happens because the Adivasis have honoured him with the title of 'Dishom Guru'. They hold him in high regard, just as people respect their parents and grandparents at home. And this respect prompts even leaders of other parties to touch his feet and seek blessings when they happen to meet him. No other Adivasi leader can claim to have such kind of respect. That's why some people call him Shibu Soren, some address him as 'Baba', some as Guruji while some others call him 'Dishom Guru'.

Launched Movement after Father's Murder

Shibu Soren was known as 'Shivlal' in his childhood. When Shivlal alias Shibu Soren was still only 13-14 years old, it had become apparent that he was different from the other boys of his age. Some of the features of his character had made it clear that he was going to attain something great in his life. Right from his childhood, he was passionate and determined; he would not listen to anybody once he made a decision. This became apparent for the first time when moneylenders killed his father. At that very moment he had vowed to take revenge and eliminate the practice of moneylending. Shibu Soren had then itself set that as the primary goal of his life and he did succeed in ultimately attaining the same. At that time, he did not even think of a separate Jharkhand state. He had only one goal - take revenge against those who had killed his father and eliminate the practice of moneylending.

Lost father in his childhood

Shibu Soren was born on 11 January 1944 in Nemra village of Gola block. Nemra at that time was in Hazaribagh district. Ramgarh district was created later and Gola became a part of Ramgarh district. Shibu Soren is second among his four brothers and two sisters. His father Sobaran Soren had made significant contributions to the freedom movement. He was a Gandhian. He laid emphasis on educating his children. Shibu Soren in his childhood was known with the names Shivlal and Shivcharan Manjhi. People in his village called him by these names only. He was admitted to a primary school in the same village. At that time, having a primary school in a village like Nemra itself was a big thing. The village did not have any facility for the next level i.e., middle and high school education. Hence, he had to be admitted to a state sponsored school at Gola. Shibu Soren stayed in an Adivasi hostel there. He used to visit his home during holidays. He was interested in sports also, and was having good time as a child.

It was 27 November 1957 when he received the bad news. The news of his father Sobaran

Young Shibu Soren

Soren's murder reached him when he was in his hostel. He immediately returned to his village. He was not able to comprehend why his father was killed. His father was a teacher and used to go to villages to promote education. He was a Gandhian and had participated in the freedom struggle also. Shibu Soren however did know that his father was against the moneylenders who were exploiting the Adivasis. The moneylenders hence did not like his father. A few incidents had taken place in the village also. Sobaran Soren had confronted some moneylenders' sons who had used some foul language for an Adivasi woman. Hence, the needle of doubt was pointing towards them only. Also, during the last rites of his father, Shibu Soren had received some leads confirming moneylenders' involvement in his father's murder. Jairam Manjhi was accompanying Sobaran Soren when the latter was murdered. He used to stay with Sobaran Soren only and helped him in his daily chores. On 27 November, Sobaran Soren and Jairam had left Nemra for Barlanga to catch a train. The route to Barlanga crossed through Narsinghdih and Sutarpur. Just as they reached Tand, the moneylenders and their men attacked Sobaran Soren. He died on the spot. Among the killers were Haribhajan Sao and Phenkan Sao, kin of Bishtu Sao of Barlanga. They had let Jairam off. He was witness to the entire incident.

Discontinued Studies

Shibu Soren was just 13 years old when his father was murdered. The incident had discomposed him. He was not in a position to concentrate on his studies. One of his father's friends even took Shibu Soren to his place for few days to enable him to recover from that tragedy and concentrate on his studies. However, this did not happen. He decided to discontinue his studies. He was aware that his father was killed only because he had been raising his voice against exploitation. Moneylenders had those days created terror in Gola and nearby areas. Innocent villagers were being badly harassed by them. These moneylenders were usurping the earnings of those villagers. They would first lend money to the villagers and then charge hefty interest at the rates going up to 500%. And in the case of non-payment, they would take over their lands. Such moneylenders had taken control of the lands of the Adivasis. They would even offer the gullible Adivasis drinks and then get their thumb impressions on papers to grab their lands. The moneylenders would forcibly take away more than half of the produce that the Adivasis harvested on their own lands. At that very tender age, Shibu Soren made up his mind that his education was not going to resolve this issue; a campaign would have to be launched against the moneylenders by bringing all the villagers together, that only would bring about their liberation from these moneylenders. But, it was not possible for him to do this alone. The youth of the village had to come forward. Shibu Soren gradually started to mobilise the youth in surrounding areas. This was not so easy.

First Step of the Movement

The terror of the moneylenders those days was so intense that none of the Adivasis were readily coming forward to stand against them. Any Adivasi raising his voice against them would get beaten up. Around that time, a bridge was being built over Gomti River on Gola-Muri Road. One Vishu Mahto of Dabhatu in Gola was being troubled by the moneylenders. Shibu Soren decided to fight against injustice and help Vishu. He supported Vishu and got him justice. This was a morale booster for Shibu Soren himself. He resolved to take this campaign further ahead. This incident prompted people to slowly come along with him. The villagers were already troubled by the moneylenders; they sensed a potential in Shibu Soren to get them free from the clutches of the moneylenders and

Bagun Sumbrui in Shibu Soren's Programme in 1970

hence, started to support him. Shibu Soren had by then understood that the moneylenders were succeeding in usurping the lands of the Adivasis because the Adivasis were illiterate and used to liquor and hariya (indigenous brew). If only the Adivasis had got educated and quit drinking, the moneylenders would not have been able to dupe them. He decided to launch a campaign against drinking also. He started this from his own home. His uncle was one day drinking hariya. Shibu Soren requested him to stop. When his uncle did not agree, he beat him up. This resulted in the reduction in sale of liquor in surrounding areas. Of course, a section of people also raised objection saying that Shibu Soren was trying to break a tradition and stop use of hariya and liquor.

Contested for the position of Mukhiya

If Shibu Soren found any exploitation or injustice at any place, he would immediately reach there along with his associates and protest. These small protests were gradually making people join him in his campaign. The faith of the villagers in him was getting stronger every day. Shibu Soren himself felt his strength and his self-confidence getting firmer. His colleagues persuaded him to contest the election for mukhiya. He contested the election for mukhiya of Barlanga panchayat, but the moneylenders colluded with the officials and managed to defeat Shibu Soren by a few votes. He did not lose heart after losing the election; instead, he adopted a more aggressive approach. He was aware that the moneylenders had occupied the lands of the Adivasis. The Adivasis were being forced to work in their own lands as labourers. He tried to make people understand that the lands belonged to their ancestors and now to them only, and the same had been grabbed by deceit. He hence exhorted people - 'If you want your land back, you would have to struggle; get ready to reclaim your lands, get your bow and arrow and start harvesting your paddy, let's see who can stop us!' People started to support him after this call. Shibu Soren, having the backing of his supporters, launched his 'cut down paddy' movement. Paddy crops were forcibly harvested from the Adivasi fields that had been grabbed by the moneylenders in Barlanga panchayat and were being used for farming by them. Young people armed with bow and arrows would surround the field where paddy crop was to be harvested and women would do the cutting. That paddy used to be then distributed among the villagers. All this helped in gradually boosting the popularity of Shibu Soren. It's not that the moneylenders kept quiet when their paddy crops were getting cut. The Police were with them and they also had their own goons. However, with Shibu Soren stood thousands of Adivasis armed with their conventional weapons. While the moneylenders' team would fire bullets, the agitators would respond with arrows. This had become a common scene there.

Constituted Santhal Navyuvak Sangh

Upliftment of the Adivasis was not possible by running the movement only around Gola; Shibu Soren hence headed towards Petarwar and Jainamore. His elder brother Raja Ram's in-laws resided in Jainamore. Shibu Soren stayed in Jilingtand at the residence of Luna Ram, father-in-law of his brother and started to organise the Adivasis there. In between, he would visit Marafari from there. Bokaro was earlier known as Marafari only. He constituted Santhal Navyuvak Sangh in the year 1962. In the meantime, he got married in 1963 to Roopi Soren of Chandil. It appeared that Shibu Soren might, after his marriage, shift his attention more towards his family than his movement. But just the reverse happened. After his marriage, Shibu Soren made his 'cut down paddy' movement more intense. At home, his wife Roopi would take care of household affairs and raise their children. Shibu Soren had gradually started to play the role of a social reformer also. He was not only fighting against the exploiters and the moneylenders but also making efforts to eliminate the evils prevalent in the Santhal communities. He was trying to bring about reforms in the society.

Constitution of Adivasi Sudhar Samiti

Shibu Soren knew that the Adivasi community could not progress until the prevalent social evils were eliminated. This required them to get educated, get rid of hariya-liquor and get united. It was not possible for him alone to achieve all this and hence, he constituted the Adivasi Sudhar Samiti in Jainamore itself. In fact, some people had usurped the land of one Putia Manjhi in Jainamore. When Shibu Soren came to know this, he reached that land and planted a flag there. The land was restored to Putia and he opened the office of Adivasi Sudhar Samiti there itself. By that time, the decision for installation of a steel plant at Bokaro was already made. Land acquisition for the same was in progress. Some walls were being erected at a few places. Shibu Soren had a friend, Alku Pandey, who was living in Kasiatand at that time. He owned a truck. Alku Pandey and

Shibu Soren would use that truck to pick bamboo at Gola and sell the same in Bokaro. Bamboo was produced in Gola in abundance. Bamboo was in high demand in Bokaro at that time. While the bamboo business was providing Shibu Soren with some earnings, he was also using this to develop contacts in Marafari. Frequent trips to Bokaro had helped him get acquainted with the Adivasi had settlements around that place.

Meeting with Dhan Singh Munda

A large number of outside contractors had arrived in Bokaro around that time to build the plant. They were outsiders. They were in control of the affairs there. This relates to the year 1968. This very year, Shibu Soren got a new and trustworthy friend in the form of Dhan Singh Munda. Dhan Singh Munda belonged to Sonua in West Singhbhum. Those days, young Adivasi boys and girls from Manoharpur, Sonua, Goilkera, Gumla, Chaibasa, Simdega and Ranchi were coming to Bokaro in search of work. Women constituted a large part of those migrants. Dhan Singh himself had come to Marafari looking for work, but the kind of things happening there was making his blood boil. He himself was just waiting for an opportunity. He himself had said this. I had gone to see Dhan Singh at his residence in Bokaro when I came to know that he had been an old friend of Shibu Soren. He was a lively and daring person. That day, he narrated an interesting story related to Shibu Soren.

Shibu Soren with Dhan Singh Munda, his old friend

Took Revenge for Teasing

In the words of Dhan Singh Munda -"Construction of the steel plant was in progress at Bokaro. The contractors of the company were mostly outsiders. The Adivasi girls and women were in the worst condition. They had come from far off places just for livelihood. They had to endure the atrocities of those contractors and their munshis for getting work from them. Many of the contractors and munshis even indulged in teasing these Adivasi women. They sometimes went to the extent of exploiting the women physically. Those women did not have any option other than keeping quiet. They used to be removed from work if they protested. The resentment was simmering below the surface. Not only the women but also male labourers were brimming with anger and were ready to take revenge. I (Dhan Singh Munda) decided to teach those outside contractors and their munshis a lesson. I made a plan for the same. I got together some 30 youths from Kasiyatand in Marafari. The Adivasis who had come from Singhbhum, Ranchi, Gumla and Simdega were staying in that very Kasiyatand colony. I arranged a meeting of the Adivasis and expressed disappointment that they were keeping quiet even though those contractors were outraging the modesty of their mothers and sisters. They should take revenge. The youth were also ready. Out of those 30 youths, I chose 12 who were ready to go to any extent to take revenge on the contractors. These Adivasi youths were capable of running very fast. I myself could run very fast, even faster than a jackal. It was felt that only a sense of fear could stop the contractors from continuing their exploitation and hence, a strategy was formulated to do something that would create a sense of terror in the minds of those contractors when they attempt any misbehaviour or exploitation. A weekly market used to be held every Tuesday there. It was decided to fix sharp-edged blades in wood pieces keeping half-a-centimetre portion of the blade exposed and use the same as weapon. It was planned to identify the contractors who indulged in exploitation and then, on the day when the weekly market was held, these contractors, when they were in the crowd, would be rapidly attacked with that weapon on their legs, backs or hands such that they got wounded and bled badly but did not die. This started happening every Tuesday. My friends and I would attack the contractors with blades. There would be commotion, and people would start shouting - catch, catch. People would even run after the youths but nobody would be able to catch them. The contractors would bleed profusely after such incidents. They started getting scared. Gradually, the effort of these Adivasi youths started showing impact. Even the contractors felt that this protest and revolt could not be suppressed by force. They gradually started to correct themselves."

People all around started talking about of Dhan Singh Munda and his friends. This fact also had come out in the open that the youths attacking the contractors were being led by Dhan Singh Munda. Even Shibu Soren had got the information that one Dhan Singh was bringing together Adivasi youths to fight against the exploitation of the Adivasis. Shibu Soren himself was doing the same thing on a larger scale. He wanted to personally find out who that Dhan Singh was and how much influence he wielded. Shibu Soren was then staying in Jainamore. He would leave Jainamore in the morning and visit the villages and settlements motivating people to come together. His impact in the region was clearly visible. Teju Mian of Jaridih and Bhola Mahto of Balidih were Shibu Soren's friends. Both of them had motorcycles. He would use any of these two motorcycles to make his trips. One day suddenly, Shibu Soren came to Kurmidih near Bokaro station. Seeing him there, people immediately started to throng around. Dhan Singh also reached there. Standing in front was Shibu Soren - fair complexioned, tall and an attractive young man with a moustache. Dhan Singh felt that Shibu Soren did not appear to be an Adivasi. People then told Dhan Singh that he only was Shibu Soren. Both were introduced to each other. Shibu Soren then asked Dhan Singh to come and meet him at Jainamore. This was their first meeting.

Dhan Singh was quite impressed in the first meeting itself. He too needed a companion to fight against the exploitation of the Adivasis. Dhan Singh also wanted to understand the modus operandi of Shibu Soren and find out who all were supporting him. With these very thoughts, he reached Jainamore to see Shibu Soren. Shibu Soren those days was running Santhal Sudhar Samiti in Jainamore. This was a social organisation that cautioned people against the evils prevalent in Santhal community; it also worked for upliftment of the Santhals. Shibu Soren told Dhan Singh about his activities and also narrated how the land of a tribal was forcibly occupied and how the same was restored and the office of Santhal Sudhar Samiti was opened on the same land. Dhan Singh immediately suggested Shibu Soren to change the name of his organisation from Santhal Sudhar Samiti to 'Adivasi Sudhar Samiti'. It was not only the Santhals but the entire Adivasi society that was suffering from exploitation and oppression. The change in the name would help people from Munda, Ho, Oraon and other Adivasi communities also to connect with this organisation. Dhan Singh Munda was becoming the voice of the Adivasis migrating from places like Singhbhum, Simdega and Gumla in search of work. Besides the Santhals, people in large numbers from the tribes like Munda, Ho and Oraon also had come from those places. Hence, Dhan Singh wanted to give a new name to Shibu Soren's organisation to enable other Adivasi communities also to connect with the same. Shibu Soren saw a point in his suggestion. He changed the name from Santhal Sudhar Samiti to Adivasi Sudhar Samiti. Dhan Singh and Shibu Soren had now come closer.

Dhan Singh now started to spend most of his time with Shibu Soren. He was now giving less time to the settlements in Bokaro. This made Dhan Singh's 12 companions believe that he did not have time for them any more and they were not going to achieve anything by continuing with him. Those youths then dissociated from Dhan Singh and got busy with their own jobs. Shibu Soren was continuously gaining strength. He had become a challenge for the moneylenders and the landlords.

Saved Life by Hiding in Haystack

It had become a common belief among the Adivasis that Shibu Soren would come to help them wherever they faced injustice. His single call would prompt people to come out of their homes armed with their conventional weapons. They would just come out, not knowing where they had to actually go. He would take his comrades to any place where there was any news of the Adivasis getting oppressed. He would eat wherever he felt hungry. There was a small hotel in Jainamore at that time - Girdhari Hotel (this hotel is now located

Shibu Soren with wife and younger son

near Chandil). He had made friends with its owner. Shibu Soren used to have his meals at that very hotel. He would pay when he had money, else he would leave without making payment. Shibu Soren was particular in one respect - he would not allow anybody else to make payment till he had enough money in his pocket. It was the time when 'cut down paddy' movement was in progress in Rukam of Petarwar. Around that time only, the landlords had made an assault on him. The moneylenders wanted to eliminate him. Not many people were accompanying Shibu Soren when this happened. Shibu Soren had somehow managed to hide in a haystack and save his life.

When his Murder was Definite

During my meeting with Dhan Singh Munda, he narrated an interesting incident related to Shibu Soren. That day, the landlords had almost killed Shibu Soren. He was fortunate to survive. He was unable to recollect the year, but this happened around 1970. That day, both Shibu Soren and Dhan Singh were returning from Petarwar side after a meeting. On the way, Ismail Miyan and his kin attacked them near Harmitta (Ulgara). This sudden attack stunned Shibu Soren. The assailants were targeting him. They caught hold of Shibu Soren but could not get Dhan Singh. Dhan Singh was standing some 100 metres away from the place where Shibu Soren was being held. He got a feeling that Ismail Miyan's family would definitely kill Shibu Soren. An idea suddenly clicked in his mind. He started shouting, 'I will not spare anybody if you even touch Shibu Soren. You better set him free.' The assailants had made a mistake. They had been unable to catch Dhan Singh. Had they caught Dhan Singh also along with Shibu Soren and had they killed both of them, nobody would have known who actually were involved in the same. Ismail Miyan had by then realised that

Dhan Singh would tell everybody if he killed Shibu Soren and then the Adivasis would not spare him. He was hence scared of the same. Their attempts to catch Dhan Singh had been futile. After much of thinking, they decided to let Shibu Soren go.

Shibu Soren had a close encounter with death that day. The moment Ismail Miyan set him free, he swiftly ran towards Dhan Singh. Both of them wanted to get away from that place as soon as possible. They were only two while the number of the assailants was many. As such, Shibu Soren was afraid Ismail Miyan might change his mind if he found both of them again. They hence wanted to reach a safe place as soon as possible. They ran up to Bagjogra in Tenughat. Sundar Manjhi stayed there. They reached his residence, had food and took some rest. They were now at a safe place. On the other side, Ismail Miyan was furious, as he had not been able to kill Shibu Soren even after capturing him. He could not endure the anger and when he next encountered a sarpanch and a tribesman, he killed them. The news of this incident soon spread everywhere.

Binod Babu saw Shibu Soren for the first time

Time was passing fast. Shibu Soren was gaining popularity all around. His area of operation also kept on getting wider gradually. Shibu Soren's activities were now not limited to Gola, Petarwar, Jainamore, Gomia and Bokaro. He had moved towards Dhanbad also. In the meantime, cases also were getting filed against him. A complaint was lodged against Shibu Soren with senior officials in Dhanbad. That very case was being heard that day. By chance, Binod Bihari Mahto and his associate A. K. Sahay were also present there. They both were lawyers. During the hearing, one of the officers had threateningly asked Shibu Soren to stop physical assaults else he would put Soren in custody. That threatening was responded by Shibu Soren in the same language, "We will continue with our action until moneylenders stop their exploitation. You may do whatever you wish." Binod Babu was listening to this conversation. Recollecting old memories, lawyer A. K. Sahay told me in a meeting with him in 2013 that after watching Shibu Soren's stance that day, Binod Babu had told him (Sahay), "This Adivasi youth has lots of guts. Keep a watch. He appears to be a man of substance." Binod Babu was a connoisseur. He had recognised Shibu Soren's strength. Though he could not have a word with Shibu Soren that day, he had understood that Shibu Soren's support might help him attain a lot of things. Land acquisition work for Bokaro Steel Plant was in progress those days.

The process of payment of compensation to raiyats was going on. Binod Bihari Mahto was running a social organisation named 'Shivaji Samaj'. This social organisation was working for upliftment of Kurmis, eradication of social evils prevalent in that community and promotion of education among them. Binod Babu was hence widely popular. Besides this, Binod Babu was also a lawyer and was active in securing compensations for raiyats. Those days, raiyats were being paid hefty sums ascompensation for acquisition of their lands by Bokaro Steel Plant. Binod Babu used to fight cases in courts to ensure raiyats were paid maximum possible compensation. In the case of a favourable verdict, the raiyat would pay as his fee a part of the compensation received. This work, many a times even involved situations leading to revolt. Discontent in the Adivasi community was also on the rise. Most of the people who were losing their lands were either Mahtos or Adivasis. Binod Babu was already a leader for the Mahtos. He had to take help from others for explaining matters to the Adivasis. He was looking for a powerful Adivasi leader. Binod Babu had heard the name of Shibu Soren. He was aware that Shibu Soren was running a social organisation in the name of 'Adivasi Sudhar Samiti' in villages around Bokaro, awakening the Adivasi community towards evils of drinking liquor and also fighting against the moneylenders. Binod Babu had also once seen Shibu Soren's mettle in the court campus. Hence, Binod Babu wanted to join hands with Shibu Soren at any cost.

Binod Babu's residence as his home

Binod Bihari Mahto (Binod Babu) was running his campaign in Dhanbad-Bokaro. He was planning to contest parliamentary election in 1971. He was aware that Shibu Soren had a good hold on Adivasi voters. Hence, he was looking for his support. For this, it was necessary for Binod Babu to meet Shibu Soren. Binod Babu thus came to Jainamore. He met Shibu Soren and also observed his work. He then asked Shibu Soren to come to Dhanbad.

Shibu Soren on the occasion of his 75th Birthday in 2019. Accompanied by Abhishek, Anuj Sinha and Hemant Soren

They were introduced to each other for the first time that day only. They had a good conversation. Shibu Soren later went to Dhanbad to meet Binod Babu. They got along so well, that Shibu Soren started living at Binod Babu's residence itself. Binod Babu contested the parliamentary election in 1971 from Dhanbad under the banner of CPM. Though he lost, Shibu Soren extended his full support in his election campaign.

Momentum for labour movement

Shibu Soren was also active in imparting momentum to the labour movement. This is an incident that occurred in October 1970. Digambar Marandi, an old associate of Shibu Soren, narrates the incident like this - "Comrade A. K. Roy was then sitting on hunger strike in Jalan Factory near Godhar colliery in Dhanbad in support of the demands of working labourers. Binod Bihari Mahto had also joined him at that time to impart momentum to the movement. One more rising leader who had arrived there was Shibu Soren. Shibu was accompanied by Teklal Mahto. Jharkhand Mukti Morcha had still not come into existence and Shibu Soren had come there in the capacity of the leader of Adivasi Sudhar Samiti. Shibu Soren's activities were at that time limited to Bokaro where steel plant was being installed. Lands were being acquired and indigenous Adivasis were getting displaced. Possibly Shibu Soren was taking part in such a session in Dhanbad for the first time. A plan was finalised in the meeting of the workers' union to launch a struggle for the cause of workers. A campaign to raise voices against exploitation was kicked off. In that meeting, people from different organisations unanimously resolved to win this fight for destabilising the empire of Panchadeo of Dhanbad (Suryadeo Singh, Sakaldeo Singh, Brahmadeo Singh, Ramdeo Singh and Narangdeo Singh). At that time, comrade A. K. Roy was running Bihar Workers Union whereas Binod Bihari Mahto was heading the organisation 'Shivaji Samaj'. On the other side, the Santhal community had formed their own organisation named 'Sonot Santhal Samaj'.

"Later, Shibu Soren also participated in the meetings of Sonot Santhal Samaj in Topchanchi-Loyabad and Damodarpur-Hirapur. Invitations for attending these meetings were sent by one government teacher Lalchand Hembram. Along with Satish Soren, I (Digambar Marandi) had also participated in those meetings. Next meeting was called in the office of Binod Bihari Mahto. Shibu Soren, N. E. Horo, comrade A. K. Roy and K. D.

Nandi - they all had arrived for the meeting on the invitation of Binod Bihari. A consensus was arrived at in that meeting for getting rid of the mafia empire. In the meanwhile, all coal mines across the country were nationalised in October 1972. Around 42000 labourers were retrenched and people were hired from Arrah, Chhapra and Balia replacing indigenous Adivasis. It was decided to fight unitedly, as that only could have safeguarded the interests of Jharkhand.

Police at the residence of Binod Babu

Shibu Soren now did not have any worries as to where he would spend his nights - he had the option to stay at the residence of Binod Babu, that also in Dhanbad. It had become easier for him now to visit nearby places. He had also got a motorcycle. Shibu Soren would make trips to Tundi and other Adivasi areas around it on that motorcycle and try to bring the Adivasis together. Around that time only, some complaint was also lodged with the Police against Shibu Soren. The police were looking for him. They knew that Shibu Soren was staying at the residence of Binod Babu. The police had even gone to Binod Babu's residence once to catch Shibu Soren but they could not get him.

❑

Formation of Jharkhand Mukti Morcha

Jharkhand Mukti Morcha is the political party that was constituted with the sole purpose of the creation of a separate Jharkhand state. It played an important role in formation of the state. Formation of Jharkhand Mukti Morcha i.e., JMM was not an instantaneous process. There is a long story behind the same. Binod Bihari Mahto, A. K. Roy and Shibu Soren along with many other people had been contemplating on its constitution for a long time. Binod Bihari Mahto, A. K. Roy and Shibu Soren were already active in the neighbouring regions of Dhanbad in different ways through different organisations and were doing a good job. Binod Bihari Mahto belonged to Dhanbad itself; he was a lawyer and a social reformer. He was running his social organisation 'Shivaji Samaj' that he had formed on 6 April 1969 in Topchanchi. In fact, Shivaji Samaj was working for the development of the Kurmi community. Besides this, it was engaged in eliminating social evils prevalent in Kurmi community and promoting education among them. He was earlier linked to CPM and had even contested parliamentary election from Dhanbad in 1971 on CPM ticket. He was quite popular in his region, especially among the Kurmi. His strong support for a separate Jharkhand state had led to his separation from CPM. After this, Binod Babu was giving his entire attention to further expand the activities of Shivaji Samaj. His area of operation had expanded beyond Dhanbad to Giridih, Bokaro and Hazaribagh.

While Binod Babu was busy in uplifting Kurmi communities and bringing awareness among them, Shibu Soren was running the campaign against moneylenders and exploiters under the banner of Adivasi Sudhar Samiti. Shibu Soren was also carrying out awareness campaigns for elimination of evils prevalent in Adivasi societies. He was also working for promoting education and community farming among Adivasis and helping them get rid of liquor. Shibu Soren was not new to Binod Babu. They had met each other when Shibu Soren had come out of Gola and had been running his movement in Bokaro and surrounding regions under the banner of Sonot Santhal Samaj. Later,

Shibu Soren was in fact staying at Binod Babu's residence only in Dhanbad for a long time and he used to make trips to Tundi and nearby areas from there. Subsequently, Shibu Soren had set up his ashram at Pokharia (Tundi). Binod Babu and Shibu Soren were in constant touch with each other and were engaged in their activities through their own social organisations. Shibu Soren and A. K. Roy would meet once in a while during that period but they did not know each other intimately at that time. Though, Binod Babu and A. K. Roy had been close to each other for a long time. They both were with CPM together. A. K. Roy was fighting for the cause of labourers in Dhanbad. Those days, people from outside Bihar were having control over the mines in Bihar (Jharkhand was yet to come into existence then). Mafia groups were dominating and labourers were being grossly exploited. A. K. Roy was an engineer in Sindri. He had left his job and was uniting the labourers and fighting against the mafias. He had earned popularity as a fighting and honest leader of the labourers.

By that time, Naxal groups had become active around Dhanbad. Around the same time, an article 'Vote and Revolution' written by A. K. Roy was published in the 'Frontier'. Publication of this article led to A. K. Roy's expulsion from CPM. After this, he was spending more of his time with the labourers. He had openly challenged the mafia. Coal mafia was also trying to teach A. K. Roy's supporters some lesson by making regular assaults on them. Many murders had taken place. He used to discuss these conditions with Binod Babu. The elections of 1972 were to be held around that time. A. K. Roy got elected as legislator from Sindri under the banner of Janwadi Sangram Samiti.

Shibu Soren's campaign against the moneylenders and his 'cut down paddy' movement had resulted in dozens of cases getting filed against him. The police were looking for him. On the other side, Binod Babu, after his separation from CPM, was thinking of forming an alternative political party. He just got a brilliant idea about teaming up with Shibu Soren to form some new political party. He thought of including A. K. Roy also in the same. Shibu Soren and Binod Babu were, in any case, already engaged in movements under different banners. A. K. Roy was quite popular among labourers because of his fighting spirit. Binod Babu discussed this subject with A. K. Roy. Finally, it was decided to call a meeting of all the three and also invite some other prominent persons to the same. Till that time, the demand for a separate Jharkhand state was not a part of any of the movements of Binod Babu, Shibu

Soren or A. K. Roy; though, they were in favour of taking the Jharkhand Movement further. They all believed that all those who were fighting for a separate state had not been successful, as, till then, it was a general perception that only Adivasis were demanding a separate Jharkhand state. If, along with the Adivasis, even non-Adivasis were included in this movement, the Jharkhand Movement could be taken to a decisive stage; and that was possible also.

A meeting was held at Binod Babu's residence in Dhanbad on 4 February 1972. It was attended by Shibu Soren, Binod Babu, A. K. Roy, Prem Prakash Hembram, erstwhile ruler of Katras Purnendu Narayan Singh, Shiva Mahto, Jadu Mahto, Shaktinath Mahto, Raj Kishore Mahto, Govind Mahto and others. A decision was taken in the meeting to merge Sonot Santhal Samaj and Shivaji Samaj and create a new organisation. Even the name for that new organisation was discussed. Many names were suggested. Bangladesh had been formed just a few months ago and Mukti Bahini had fought a long battle for the same. Vietnam was also going through a movement. Linking with the struggle at both the places, it was decided to name the new organisation as 'Jharkhand Mukti Morcha'. There itself, the central committee of Jharkhand Mukti Morcha was also constituted.

Unanimously, Binod Bihari Mahto and Shibu Soren were designated as the President and the General Secretary respectively. Purnendu Narayan Singh was selected as the Vice President, Teklal Mahto (Topchanchi) as the Secretary and Chudamani Mahto as the Treasurer. Shankar Kishore Mahto was designated as the Office Secretary.

First Foundation Day Celebrated in 1973

The formation of Jharkhand Mukti Morcha had provided Shibu Soren an opportunity to demonstrate his power. Till then, Shibu Soren's campaigns were limited to 'cut down paddy' movement and operations against the moneylenders only. He had not got any opportunity to demonstrate his capability in a city. Now he had the backing of an organisation like JMM. The Jharkhand Mukti Morcha had celebrated its first Foundation Day publicly on 4 February 1973 at Golf Ground in Dhanbad. This was a historical event. For the first time, a meeting of around a lakh of people was organised on the soil of Dhanbad demanding a separate Jharkhand state. It was winter then. The organisers had arranged to drop several truckloads of coal all around the ground to ensure some relief from cold for the people attending the meeting. Besides people from Dhanbad, Adivasis from

Giridih, Hazaribagh, Jamtara and Deoghar had also attended the meeting with their traditional costumes and arms. The meeting ground was filled with red and green flags. Before this, all the meetings or rallies that Binod Babu had organised used to have more of Kurmis and non-Adivasis, but this formation of Jharkhand Mukti Morcha and Shibu Soren's involvement in the same had considerably attracted the Adivasis. Adivasis had come to the meeting barefoot from far off places. A. K. Roy's involvement had led to participation in the rally by labourers in large numbers.

Shibu Soren with old friends Nirmal Mahto, Shailendra Mahto

Mukut Bihari Singh, the editor of 'Yugantar' at that time was a freedom fighter and had a thorough grasp and extensive understanding of the politics around Dhanbad. He was personally present at the venue of the first Foundation Day of JMM. He published a lively description of the entire session and the environment there on the day. Mukut Babu writes, "It may be around 1 O'clock in the afternoon. A sound of drumbeats appeared to be approaching from the north side. It attracted our attention and we found a large group of people in the form of a procession marching towards us. The procession appeared to be slowly inching towards Golf Ground and its first contingent managed to enter the ground in around half an hour. The stream of that procession looked never-ending and the swarm of those Adivasi protestors including some local indigenous residents kept on spreading across the ground in a thoroughly peaceful and organised manner. They were in their traditional attire. With their bundles of foodstuff and cloth to cover themselves on their back, they kept on arriving, swaying with joy. Around the same time, we heard the chanting of 'Inquilab Zindabad' from the other side, and we found the coal mine labourers, led by the colleagues of A. K. Roy, entering the ground flaunting their red flags. Batch after batch of labourers kept on arriving and spreading all across the ground merging with the Adivasis and the villagers there. It was a rare and encouraging scene; that scene of the union of farmers and labourers. Every face was beaming with enthusiasm and self-confidence, a desire to sacrifice everything for one's rights, a feeling of 'do or die'."

It has been a peculiarity of Jharkhand Mukti Morcha that all of their rallies of this kind usually start late and go on till late in the night. That rally of 1973 also followed the same pattern. The meeting started late in the evening and went on till late night. Shibu Soren proposed the name of Binod Babu as the chairman of the meeting. The entire ground was reverberating with chants of 'Shibu Soren, Binod Bihari Mahto and A. K. Roy Zindabad'. The overwhelming strength of JMM was visible for the first time. N. E. Horo also had been invited to the rally. He was already a parliamentarian from Jharkhand Party at that time. He had even delivered a speech. A. K. Roy also had delivered a speech and had announced that the union of green flag and red flag had set in motion a movement against exploitation and oppression. General Secretary Shibu Soren also presented the agenda of Jharkhand Mukti Morcha and called upon the people to spread the same to all the villages. The round of speeches went on for the whole night. The people attending the rally held on despite chilling cold. Next day, the workers armed with traditional weapons took out a procession from the Golf Ground and after passing through Jharia, Putki and Karkend, returned to the ground. The total distance was over 20 km and the workers had travelled the entire distance on foot. While entering Jharia, this procession of the Adivasis with bows and arrows and other traditional weapons had created a sense of fear there. The shops were closed but the procession crossed the town peacefully. The rally instilled a sense of enthusiasm in the movement for Jharkhand state in the entire Chhotanagpur region. Jharkhand Mukti Morcha reaped immense benefits from this historical rally.

Shibu Soren dodged the Police

Jharkhand Mukti Morcha had become quite active after its Dhanbad rally on 4 February 1973. Shibu Soren was actively carrying out his work in Tundi-Pirtand region. The 'cut down paddy' movement had gained momentum. Shibu Soren and his colleagues were taking action against the moneylenders. With the same speed, cases were being lodged in various police stations against Shibu Soren. By the time the next Foundation Day (4 February 1974) arrived, dozens of cases were already lodged against Shibu Soren and the police were looking for him. A large area right from Pirtand-Tundi to Raniganj had been turned into a liberated region where Shibu Soren was running a parallel government. That entire region was a liberated region. The police would not easily dare to enter that region and when they did try, Shibu Soren would get prior information about the same. Shibu Soren was then the General Secretary of JMM. The police were looking for him and hence, he was not in a position to carry out his activities in Dhanbad openly. The police had already arrested President Binod Babu under the Internal Security Act and he was at that time lodged in Patna Central jail. In the circumstances, it was a major challenge for the party to arrange a rally and celebrate the Foundation Day of Jharkhand Mukti Morcha. Finally, it was decided to organise the Foundation Day function under any circumstances on 4 February only in Dhanbad. Everybody had assumed that Shibu Soren would not attend this programme as the police was on the look-out for him. Despite that, a large crowd had gathered there. The police also were posted in a large number so as to arrest Shibu Soren just in case he turned up there. The meeting was held in the night. Some speech was in progress. Suddenly Shibu Soren appeared on the stage. The police were just waiting for the meeting to end to arrest him. Arresting him on the stage would have resulted in violent reactions from JMM workers and it would have been difficult to manage the same. The same Shibu Soren who was absconding and whom the police were looking for stepped onto the stage in a programme organised right in the middle of Dhanbad city and also delivered a speech. At the end of the programme, when the police came to the stage to arrest him, they had to return empty handed. Shibu Soren had already got away dodging the police. Before the police could capture him in Dhanbad, he had reached his liberated region.

Dodged the Police in Ranchi also

It's not that Shibu Soren had dodged the police in Dhanbad only. Some incidents had occurred earlier also when the police were just waiting to arrest Shibu Soren and he had managed to slip away. One such incident relates to 16 December 1993. It was the time when the economic blockage was in progress. It was the first day. Both Shibu Soren and Suraj Mandal were interacting with journalists in Chinar Hotel at Ranchi. They both were Members of Parliament at that time. Shibu Soren had two bodyguards. Officers from intelligence department as well as many police personnel were present there to keep a watch on Shibu Soren. However, Shibu Soren had, the previous day itself, found out an alternative passage to reach his room in Hotel Chinar and also to come out to the location where he planned to meet the journalists. That is to say, he had made his plans on the previous day itself as to how he could get away from there dodging the police. After the journalists left at the end of their session with him, Shibu Soren got away with his bodyguards through the back door. To mislead the police, he did not even use his personal vehicle parked outside the hotel. He even left Suraj Mandal in the hotel itself for two hours. The police kept waiting outside for Shibu Soren to come out of the hotel. When Suraj Mandal came out, Shibu Soren was not with him. The police sensed something fishy. By that time, Shibu Soren was far away from their reach. In fact, the police feared that the economic blockage might turn violent and that was the reason he was being kept under observation.

Shibu Soren's Struggle in Tundi

It was Shibu Soren's struggle in Tundi that has been the most important struggle of his life. This was the struggle that provided him an identity on national level. Shibu Soren had close encounters with death on many occasions in the course of that struggle. The police were hunting for him and he even had an award on his head. Besides that, even moneylenders, pawnbrokers and landlords were gunning for his life. However, eluding all of them, Shibu Soren did carry out his programmes in Tundi and nearby areas in a way that had prompted many prominent journalists to visit the region and have a first-hand look at the same. Those days, Shibu Soren was not only fighting against the moneylenders but also working as a social reformist. His programmes for prohibition, community farming, night schools, goat and pig farming and land restoration had helped the

Adivasis to gradually become self-reliant. He was enjoying massive support from the Adivasis. Adivasi people armed with bows and arrows used to be always around him to ensure his safety. It was Shibu Soren's struggle in Tundi only that was so impressive that it made the then Prime Minister Indira Gandhi notice him and later he even got the opportunity to have a meeting with Indira Ji.

Tundi's Movement Provided an Identity

As such, Shibu Soren had been, for a long time, running his movement against moneylenders and landlords along with his social-reform campaigns in Gola, Petarwar, Jainamore, Bokaro, Dhanbad and neighbouring areas, but the movement that he led from 1972 to 1976 was so effective that the same made him widely known. The Adivasis would acclaim him while his name itself would scare the moneylenders. There was a sense of fear among the moneylenders and the landlords. The movement was enabling restoration of lands that had been taken over by the moneylenders, to their original Adivasi owners. The Adivasis used to be properly armed with their traditional weapons i.e., bows and arrows while harvesting their produce in the fields. The male Adivasis would stand and guard all around the field while females would cut paddy. In case of any protest or any firing from the side of the moneylenders, those Adivasis all around the field would rain down arrows on them. Even though the moneylenders cultivated the lands they had usurped from the Adivasis, the Adivasis would come when the crop got ready and forcibly cut the same as their revenge. They used to do this as those lands belonged to their ancestors.

Tundi-a Safe Location

Though this movement had gained momentum in 1972, it had taken some time to create the foundation for the same. Shibu Soren himself had to work hard for a long time for this. Right from the days when Shibu Soren was staying in Dhanbad, he had started making efforts to unite the Adivasis in the tribal areas of Dhanbad and Giridih for their fight against the moneylending system and exploitation by the landlords. He used to visit Tundi in this regard. That was not a small place. While Tundi is located on one side of Parasnath hills, Pirtand is on the other side. One falls in Dhanbad district while the other is in Giridih.

Shibu Soren knew that the fight against the moneylenders and the landlords was not going to be easy and the same would run long. A safe location was needed to be used as a base to run a protracted movement. This location was expected to be beyond the reach of the police. He considered Tundi suitable for this for many reasons. That the Adivasis in Tundi and surrounding villages were being badly harassed by the landlords and the moneylenders there was one of the reasons. The Adivasis were already harbouring resentment against them for quite some time but they were unable to launch a struggle in the absence of a leadership. The second main reason was the demography there - Tundi was predominantly an Adivasi, especially Santhal populated area. The third reason was its geographical character. It was surrounded by dense forests and was located close to Parasnath hills. Shibu Soren was already under police surveillance because of the violent protests in Dhanbad, Bokaro and nearby areas. The police were even looking for him. Shibu Soren was aware that it was easy for the police to arrest him in Dhanbad or Bokaro but it was too difficult for them to enter the forests of Tundi or Parasnath. Even if they entered the forests, it would not have been possible for them to arrest him. Considering all these facts, Shibu Soren had chosen Tundi area as his safe harbour. He had a motorcycle that he earlier used to make trips to Tundi when he was in Dhanbad. Tundi is at a distance of around 35 km only from Dhanbad. He would leave Dhanbad early in the morning and conduct meetings at different villages to awaken the Adivasis before returning to Dhanbad in the night. He was staying at the residence of Binod Babu (Binod Bihari Mahto) in Dhanbad. Though Tundi was not too far from Dhanbad, it was quite isolated and neglected. Initially, he used to go there every day early morning on his motorcycle and return by late evening or in the night. He was in any case familiar with every inch of the area. Recollecting the old memories, Dhan Singh Munda, his companion in the movement, had mentioned that sometimes Shibu Soren did not return to Dhanbad even for three-four days. He would visit one village after another and carry on with his campaign to bring together people in those villages. He would spend his night in one of those villages.

Stayed at Khokha's Residence in Palma

Shibu Soren had decided to stay near Tundi only and carry on his movement from there. For this, he selected a place called Palma located in the midst of dense forests and hills. There was one sorcerer Suku Murmu in Palma; he was called by the name 'Khokha'. Shibu Soren started staying in his house. After staying there for a few months, he moved to Muni Lal's residence. Muni Lal was a teacher. Shibu Soren started to unite the Adivasis in surrounding areas. The people there had given a rousing welcome to Shibu Soren. They were already familiar with him. Shibu Soren commanded such an overwhelming influence there that his single call used to make thousands of Adivasis assemble together with their bows and arrows. The Adivasis there had full faith in Shibu Soren. Santhals believed that this was the person who could get them out of the clutches of the moneylenders and the landlords and restore their lands to them. That entire area had been suffering from the atrocities of the moneylenders and the landlords for a long time. Most of the Adivasis were illiterate and they lacked awareness. They had become addicted to *hariya* and liquor. The moneylenders would take advantage of the same and take control of their lands after making them drunk. Poverty was already prevalent there. The moneylenders would get these Adivasis entangled in the net of their loans and charge interest at the rates going up to 500%. People were just getting ruined. Shibu Soren had resolved to first of all make the Adivasis aware, get them rid of *hariya* and liquor and then fight for restoration of their lands. Though Shibu Soren was staying in Tundi, the impact of his movement had started to become visible even in the villages of Dhanbad, Giridih and Hazaribagh.

Police Firing, Four Dead

As such, Palma was a village situated in the midst of Parasnath hills where even the police hesitated to enter. However, it was in this very Palma village where the police had once tried to target Shibu Soren. Shibu Soren was not in the village at that time, but the police action had resulted in death of four of his associates. This happened on 23 March 1972. A meeting against the moneylenders was in progress in Palma village. These kinds of meetings only decided the next moneylender to be targeted or the next landlord whose paddy crop was to be cut. The meetings used to be kept secret. The Adivasis used to convey notice of the same in their own way (by tying leaves with sticks). Around 400 Adivasis were there in that meeting. Shibu Soren used to keep making trips to various villages in the entire region. He was about to reach Palma for that meeting; but in the meanwhile, the police somehow came to know about the meeting and they reached there with a large contingent. This resulted in a commotion there. The police started firing and the Adivasis responded with their arrows. The police had come fully prepared whereas Shibu Soren's companions were not well prepared for this. The villagers hence got scared after police action and they started to run here and there. The police started firing on the fleeing Adivasis. This resulted in death of four of Shibu Soren's companions - Amulya Sen, Ratilal Murmu, Sagar Soren and Bali Miyan. They all had been with Guruji right from the days when he had first launched his movement in Tundi region.

When Even the Moneylenders Supported Shibu Soren

Maniadih is very close to Tundi. This was the place where Shibu Soren had launched his first campaign against the moneylenders. There was one Murlidhar there. Santhals, under the leadership of Shibu Soren had taken control of his land. They had even cut down his paddy crop. Murlidhar was left with no stock of grains. He had then decided to join Shibu Soren's movement. Recollecting old memories, Murlidhar had, in 2012 at his residence in Maniadih, narrated an interesting story. Murlidhar is the same person whose land was the first to be taken over by Shibu Soren and his supporters; later, Shibu Soren had himself assumed responsibility for education of his younger brother. He arranged for his education and made him a lawyer and later, even helped him get a seat in the Rajya Sabha. This is a story of nobody else but Sanjeev Kumar. This is in any case a separate and long story. Before that, it's necessary to understand fully how a moneylender's family decided to join the movement. The Adivasis were already quite agitated after the incident of firing

Murlidhar of Maniyadih was a moneylender, later joined Shibu Soren in his movement

from the moneylenders' side. Alongside, the 'cut down paddy' movement was also in full swing. Murlidhar's land also had been taken over. The food grains had already been looted. In that situation, Murlidhar, one day, made up his mind to take the risk and meet Shibu Soren. Shibu Soren was then staying at the residence of Chhatiklal in Bandhdih. He was sitting on a cot. Murlidhar reached there. Hundreds of Santhals armed with their bows and arrows were standing around Shibu Soren. The moment they saw Murlidhar, they started uttering that a moneylender's son had arrived and he ought to be killed. Murlidhar for a moment thought he was going to lose his life, but what actually happened was just the reverse. Before the Santhals could do anything, Shibu Soren intervened and asked people not to do any harm to him. Shibu Soren offered Murlidhar a seat on the cot next to him and impressed upon the Santhals to restrict the fight for the farms to the farms only. He persuaded them to listen to what he had to say. Shibu Soren offered him a cigarette. Murlidhar was quite nervous and was shivering with fear. Shibu Soren asked him, "What brings you here?"

"We don't have anything left now. You have taken everything from us. We want to join your movement," responded Murlidhar.

Shibu Soren did not believe him; why would a moneylender's son join 'cut down paddy' movement? There was one more reason for him to doubt Murlidhar. The same Murlidhar had lost everything - land, crops etc. in that movement; why would such a person support him? For once, Shibu Soren wondered if there was some politics involved in the same or the moneylender was planning something. All these questions were flashing in the mind of Shibu Soren. Despite that, he told Murlidhar to join the movement if he was really so eager for the same. Murlidhar agreed. The Santhals present there were not able to comprehend what was going on, as this was the first such incident where a moneylender's son himself was standing in support of the 'cut down paddy' movement.

When I met Murlidhar at his residence, I had asked him after all why did he choose to support Shibu Soren? Was it out of fear or did he really feel that the movement was right? Murlidhar had then explained, "There was no other way out at that time. We had lost everything. This was the best option that I could think of then. Otherwise also, there was a feeling somewhere inside that a lot of injustice had been done to the Adivasis."

Murlidhar, after getting the green signal from Shibu Soren, returned to his home. Next day, he again went to Shibu Soren with some halwa that he had got prepared at home. The halwa was meant for Shibu Soren. Murlidhar knew that Shibu Soren and his supporters would surely doubt his intentions, and hence he first tasted some halwa from the pot and then only offered the same to Shibu Soren. He did so to convince Shibu Soren that the halwa was free from any contamination. Shibu Soren had the halwa with pleasure; from that very day, he started to trust Murlidhar. Thus, a moneylender's son had become an agitator. Shibu Soren was constantly getting stronger.

Maniadih: Shibu had pacified the enraged Santhals

This incident took place at Maniadih in November 1973. The 'cut down paddy' movement had become popular by then. In many of the areas, the Adivasis had on their own, even in the absence of Shibu Soren, started cutting crops in the fields that belonged to them earlier and that had been taken over by the moneylenders. The moneylenders were holding many of the farms as mortgage. The Adivasis had started cutting paddy crops in all such fields. The moneylenders were powerful. They even protested against this during initial days. Some incidents of encounters had also taken place. Paddy cutting was in progress in Nawadah, Maniadih and Shitalpur. The moneylenders initially protested against the same, but later invited the Adivasis to Maniadih for talks. The Adivasis did not have any senior leader with them at that time. The moneylenders had made all arrangements. The meeting was arranged in

Jaherthan near Maniadih. The moneylenders had come fully prepared. The Adivasis had not been able to sense their ploy. The moneylenders there asked the Adivasis to stop cutting crops. The Adivasis (they were mostly Santhals) refused to comply with their instruction and insisted on cutting the standing crops in any case. The situation got tense; meanwhile, the moneylenders opened fire on the Santhals. One of the bullets hit Babulal Baske of Goidaha village. He was covered in blood. Two other Santhals also were injured but the condition of Babulal Baske was the worst. The news of the firing was conveyed without any delay to nearby villages by beating nagadas and dugdugis. The sound of Santhals' nagadas started reverberating all around and people were asked to march towards Jaherthan. Within two-three hours, before their eyes, more than 1000 Santhals gathered there armed with their traditional weapons. This incident had taken place around 10-11 O'clock. Shibu Soren was in Palma at that time. He also got the news of the firing. He rushed to Maniadih. He found the Santhals quite enraged there. They were standing around Babulal Baske covered in blood. Shibu Soren's presence doubled the Santhals' strength. They were adamant on taking revenge. The Santhals wanted to attack the moneylenders' houses. Shibu Soren was trying to pacify them but nobody was ready to listen to him. The Santhals were insisting to take revenge by blood for blood and not to spare even a single diku. Shibu Soren knew that this could lead to a major incident if the crowd was not controlled. He tried hard to pacify the Santhals but nobody was ready to calm down. They were even not ready to take Babulal Baske for treatment. The Santhals wanted Shibu Soren to give them the order to attack the moneylenders' houses and kill them. Shibu Soren was aware that there were only 3-4 moneylenders in the village and the rest were only poor dikus who were outsiders settled there but were not harming anybody. If the Santhals went ahead with the assault, even those innocent dikus might get killed along with the moneylenders. Shibu Soren was finding himself helpless. The same Santhals, who used to be always ready to risk their lives at his single call, on seeing Babulal injured, were too enraged to even listen to Shibu Soren's pleas. Understanding the situation, Shibu Soren tried to divert the attention to something else. He knew that the situation, if left uncontrolled, could take any ugly turn. He told the Santhals that it was the government who had provided the guns to the moneylenders and hence it was more appropriate to go for a gherao of the police station and register their protest there. The Santhals agreed to his suggestion. They all started to march towards the police station. The Santhals were armed with their traditional weapons. Their number was continuously increasing. By the time they reached the police station, the number had gone up to 8 to 10 thousand. The demonstration went on for hours. This gherao went on for a long time and that brought down the anger of the Santhals. By the time it was night, all the Santhals were back to their homes. Thus, Shibu Soren's foresight had avoided a major tragedy.

Kurko: Three of Guruji's associates killed in police firing

Shibu Soren's movement had spread to places outside Tundi's surrounding areas right after 1972. The Adivasis would meet in every village and resolve to reclaim their lands from the moneylenders. The Adivasis felt convinced that it was only Shibu Soren who could restore their ancestors' lands that the moneylenders had taken over. People had started to identify the moneylenders. Kurko falls under the Pirtand area of Giridih. This happened on 15 April 1974. The villagers held a meeting where people complained that the moneylenders were not only seizing their lands but also taking away their goats;

they needed to be taught a lesson. The villagers accused Chudo Singh, Khirodhar Rai and Budhan Rai of exploiting the Adivasis and taking away their goats. After the meeting, the Adivasis armed with their traditional weapons surrounded the houses of all the three, dragged them out of their houses and beat them to death. As the Adivasis were in large numbers, the moneylenders and their supporters could not do anything.

The mukhiya informed the police about the incident. The villagers never expected the police to come there. Finding the police there, the villagers started attacking them with arrows. Both the sides started attacking each other - firing from one side and arrows from the other side. The villagers also ran here and there to save themselves from the bullets. Three villagers - Dhansu Rai, Sonara Tudu and Gopal Mahto lost their lives in the incident. Shibu Soren was not present there at that time but eight persons including him were made accused in the FIR. A charge sheet against Shibu Soren was filed in the case in 1978. Most of the accused were acquitted in 1986. This case came up for hearing again after formation of Jharkhand state. Shibu Soren had to present himself in the court. The Additional District Judge of Giridih acquitted him in this murder case on 15 June 2010.

Police inspector killed in Topchanchi

The Jharkhand Movement did have some incidents where policemen got killed, but they were mostly constables only. The first incident involving the death of a police inspector resulting from the Jharkhand Movement occurred in 1974 at Topchanchi. A few days back, Binod Babu and Shibu Soren had organised a meeting there. They had even delivered powerful speeches. The villagers were also high-spirited. The police had filed a complaint against some Santhals in a case relating to a village near Topchanchi. Some Santhals had been arrested and it was told that they would be released after questioning. However, they were not released. The police had also visited the village. Only a few days ago, the Superintendent of Police of Dhanbad had deputed an inspector (his name was Ghatak) to Topchanchi for collecting information. That inspector had been promoted recently. The police team that had gone to the village included Ghatak also. Other members in the team included one ASI Sampat Rai and some constables. When the villagers came to know that the police were in the village for making arrests, they tried to corner them. Sampat Rai and all the constables somehow managed to escape and save their lives, but the villagers were successful in catching inspector Ghatak. He could not be traced after that. The news of the inspector getting kidnapped was flashed everywhere. The Bihar government was shaken. An order was also issued not to use force as that might put the inspector's life in danger. An additional police team was also deputed to search for the inspector but he could not be traced. Even the senior leaders of the movement were questioned but still there was no result. Even the body of the inspector could not be traced. Later, there was some news of his burnt badge having been found in the dense forests. This was the first incident of a police inspector getting killed in the course of the Jharkhand Movement. Police activities in the entire area had gone up after the murder of inspector Ghatak. The police wanted to arrest Binod Babu and Shibu Soren. Unlimited powers were provided to the police and there was instruction to shoot Shibu Soren at sight. A few days later, Binod Babu was arrested under MISA and lodged in jail.

Shibu Soren had encircled Giridih

Shibu Soren had become quite powerful around the time when the incident involving the inspector's murder took place. He was in control of the entire area around Tundi. Shibu Soren had proclaimed the entire area a liberated area. Nobody could enter or exit this area without his permission. The police did not even dare to reach near his bases located in the Parasnath hills. Even government officials and employees did not go there. This immense power of Shibu Soren was in the news outside as well. However, he made the world realise his immense power for the first time when he surrounded a large part of Giridih town demanding release of Binod Bihari Mahto. He was accompanied by over 20000 Adivasis armed with bows and arrows and other traditional weapons. This incident happened in December 1974. A few days back only, an enraged crowd had killed the inspector of Topchanchi. The then president of Jharkhand Mukti Morcha Binod Bihari Mahto was made accused in the same case. He was charged for instigating the Adivasis to kill the inspector. He was arrested for the same and lodged in Giridih jail. He had been in jail for a long time. All attempts to get him released had failed. The district administration was in no mood to set him free at any cost and was going on filing case after case against him. Shibu Soren and his supporters had understood that it was not easy to get Binod Babu released and the government was bent upon keeping him in jail at any cost. Hence, he prepared for getting him freed by force. He had considerable influence in Hazaribagh, Giridih,

Dhanbad and Santhal Pargana. He directed the Adivasis in all these districts to march to Giridih town. The Adivasis in large numbers from all these places reached Giridih on foot only. The number of Adivasis was estimated to be over 20000. The entire town of Giridih was terrorised. The town was experiencing this kind of a protest for the first time. People were also apprehensive of some untoward incident. Shibu Soren's supporters had reached major crossings of the town. The protesters were however quite disciplined and had assembled in a peaceful manner in PWD ground in front of Giridih jail. Shibu Soren was leading them.

The administration had prior knowledge of the same and it was well prepared. The district administration had the information that the Adivasis' mob might ransack the jail and get Binod Bihari Mahto out. Hence, policemen armed with Sten guns were posted on the main door of the jail. The protesters were chanting the slogan 'Jail ka tala tutega' (Jail locks will be broken, Binod Bihari will be freed). The district administration was aware that any use of force would have incited the protesters and it would have been difficult to control the situation arising out of the same. Hence, the officials wanted to pacify them and send them back. The then Deputy Commissioner also worked with patience and informed Shibu Soren that Binod Babu had already been shifted to Bhagalpur jail. He was not in Giridih jail and hence the administration was not in a position to do anything. And it was correct also. The administration had got prior information that Shibu Soren was planning to come with a large number of his Adivasi supporters to get Binod Babu released. The decision to shift Binod Babu to Bhagalpur jail was taken at that very moment. The Deputy Commissioner's words had impact on Shibu Soren. He also had the information that Binod Babu had been shifted from Giridih jail. Hence, after the protest, he ended the meeting and asked the protesters to peacefully return to their places. The protesters followed and returned but Shibu Soren was successful in making the government realise his strength.

Ashram in Pokharia

Shibu Soren used to spend most of his time in Palma. As his area of operation had expanded, he decided to stay in Tundi instead of a far-off location. He had even started to make trips to Santhal Pargana. He was running a number of development schemes in nearby villages and hence, he was finding it difficult to pay attention to

The Ashram in Pokhariya near Tundi, from where Shibu Soren conducted his movement

all of them from Palma. He made Pokharia his new base. People started to call the house where he was staying as 'Shibu Ashram'. Now, even Shibu Soren's old friend Dhan Singh Munda was making fewer trips from Dhanbad-Bokaro. Some youths in Pokharia gradually started getting closer to him. Shibu Soren's new team was ready. This included Rajendra Prasad Tiwari of Purnadih, Kripal Singh of Maniadih, Kinu Murmu of Alkusia, Koswa Tudu of Pithaldih, Basant Pathak and Jhagru Pandit etc. Till now, Shibu Soren was staying at the house of a colleague. Earlier also, he used to frequently visit Badoli Murmu in Pokharia. Shibu Soren treated Badoli as his mother. Badoli herself used to treat and feed Shibu Soren as her son.

Shibu Soren had started his 'ashram' at her house only. Badoli Murmu's son Shyam Lal Murmu was involved in the movement with Shibu Soren. He used to style his hair similar to that of Shibu Soren those days. Thus, the 'ashram' became the centre of the movement.

Guruji's Associates in Tundi

It's true that Shibu Soren was successful in every movement that he launched; however, his associates also had made major contributions to his accomplishment. Be it the struggle related to Gola to Bokaro or Bokaro to Dhanbad-Tundi or Santhal Pargana, Guruji had the privilege of having trustworthy associates everywhere. They always supported Shibu Soren on his single call without any self-interest. Their number may run in hundreds, but there were some associates who had been assigned major responsibilities by Shibu Soren. That list even included workers like Durga Tiwari who took upon himself the blame of a murder and went to jail while Shibu Soren and Binod Bihari Mahto were actually made accused in the case. The number of people making sacrifices of that level is quite small.

During the days when Shibu Soren was running his movement and carrying out activities against the moneylenders, many of his opponents also used to keep looking for opportunities. The police also were after him. In the circumstances, Shibu Soren's associates and his supporters used to be always ready to protect him. In Palma, Adivasi youths armed with bows and arrows would constantly maintain security for him. However, Basant Pathak, Jhagru Pandit, Kripal Singh, Rajendra Tiwari, Shyam Lal Murmu and Prakash were the people who would implement his schemes and also protect him from all the troubles.

Kripal Singh

Kripal Singh is one the prominent individuals in the team of Shibu Soren. The story of his joining the movement is also quite interesting. Veer Bharat Talwar had visited Shibu Soren's ashram in 1975. At that time , he had come to know of some interesting details about Kripal Singh and he had made a note of the same in his diary. In fact, Kripal Singh was once a staunch opponent of Shibu Soren and his movement. He himself was a Ghatwar. Shibu Soren was running his campaign against the moneylenders and pawnbrokers. The moneylenders had even attempted to colour Shibu Soren's (Guruji) movement as a movement of the Santhals against non-Adivasis. The moneylenders used to organise large meetings for the same. During the initial days, Kripal Singh would be assigned the responsibility of mobilising people for the meetings organised in protest of Shibu Soren's movement. While on one side, his movement was fast spreading all around, on the other side, the group of moneylenders was also actively working to stop the movement and lessen the impact of the same. The moneylenders' organisation was known as 'Kisan-Majdoor Suraksha Samiti, Chhotanagpur' (Tundi Branch). Kripal Singh used to publicise the organisation and mobilise people by beating drums. Kripal Singh had a friend named Jaideo Prasad Singh Chaudhary. He was not a moneylender himself but was engaged in promoting the ideas of the moneylenders. He would oppose Shibu Soren openly and win acclaim for the same. The moneylenders were using Kripal Singh for their self-interest. There were instances when Kripal Singh and Jaideo Prasad led the protests of the moneylenders at DC office and tried to convey that the Adivasis under the leadership of Shibu Soren had created terror in the region. The moneylenders' Samiti had once organised a large meeting attended by over 20000 people at Maniadih. This provides an idea of the strength of the people Shibu Soren and his associates were fighting against. It was publicised in that meeting that Shibu Soren was fighting against not only the moneylenders but also all non-Adivasis. The moneylenders got so excited to see the crowd that they brought in many proposals. According to one of the proposals, the supporters of the Samiti were to assemble in large number at a place and go about ransacking and burning down the houses of the Adivasis and killing them. Another proposal suggested stopping sale of any item to the Adivasis at the shops of the moneylenders and dikus. This proposal was even implemented for some time; however, as this resulted in loss to the moneylenders and hawkers, the proposal was withdrawn. Kripal Singh would attend all such meetings but he always felt some reluctance in his mind.

Kripal Singh started to feel that the moneylenders were exploiting the Adivasis. He was in a dilemma. In the meantime, he happened to meet Narad Sen. Narad told him that Shibu Soren's movement was good. Guruji believed in non-violence and he was fighting for the independence of Jharkhand. He should be supported. After this, Kripal Singh started to have some change in perception. His impressions of Shibu Soren started undergoing change. He gained faith in Guruji and he kept silent after that. This happened in February 1974. He then went out for six months. By the time Kripal Singh returned, everything had changed.

In fact, during 1974, the moneylenders initially tried to suppress Shibu Soren's movement and even made assault attempts; however, as the time passed, Shibu Soren went on gaining strength. The Adivasis started to reclaim the lands that the moneylenders had somehow managed to take over from them. After that, Kripal Singh decided to work with Guruji. He belonged to a poor family and earned his livelihood from tuitions. Guruji was impressed by his work and he brought Kripal into his core team. Kripal had studied up to matriculation from Tundi High School. Guruji hence assigned him the responsibility of teaching. He became the teacher of Akil Akhara and became a prominent associate of Guruji in his campaign to make people literate. This campaign by Guruji was quite successful.

Basant Pathak

Basant Pathak is considered to be one of the oldest associates of Shibu Soren's movement. Basant was aggressive in nature right from his childhood. He never tolerated injustice. He is one of those non-Adivasis who were with Shibu Soren during initial days of his movement. At the time, the general perception was that Guruji was a leader of the Adivasis and was fighting for them only. Basant's father, Janki Pathak was a vaidya and lived in Gandey block of Giridih. He even conducted pooja rituals sometimes. He was a Congress supporter. Basant was quite opposite to him in nature. He hated the rich. Whenever rich students in his hostel used to bring beaten rice or other nice foodstuff, he would snatch the same from them. The school had caste-based politics even at that time. In one of such controversies, he even went to the extent of beating the teacher who troubled him using caste politics. He was put in jail for one and a half months. Even the headmaster of his school used to expel students. He was afraid the headmaster might expel him also from the school.

Basant Pathak, Shibu Soren's Associate

Once out of jail, Basant went to the headmaster with a knife in his hand. He even attacked him with the knife. He was sent to jail again. Basant was convicted. He beat the Magistrate who pronounced the judgement. He again went to jail, also paid the fine. After he was released, he came to know that Shibu Soren was running a movement against moneylenders. Basant himself was against the exploiters. Hence, he met Shibu Soren and joined his movement. The above incidents indicate the kind of temperament Basant had.

Basant was staying with Guruji in Pokharia ashram. Though he had studied up to matriculation only, he was adept at writing revolutionary songs. He had earned the confidence of Guruji in a very short time. Guruji was aware of Basant's strength and hence he chose to assign him a job that was fit for him. Guruji knew that Basant was strong physically also; he hence made Basant his lieutenant. He would always be there for Guruji's security. This was the time when Guruji was running his parallel government in Tundi. His revolutionary songs had helped Guruji a lot in mobilising the Adivasis against the moneylenders and also in creating a sense of fear among the moneylenders. One of his songs goes as below.

Jago-Jago re Majdoor

Jago-Jago re Kisan

Are, Jharkhand Mata Mang rhi

Veeron ka Balidan

Jago-Jago re Majdoor.....
Are, Mahajanon ke sir ko kato
Looto Khet Khalihan

Jago-Jago re Majdoor.........
Are, Sabhi Varg ke Lango Jago
Looto Ghar-Makan

Jago-Jago re Majdoor....
Are, Mukti morcha mang raha
Veeron ke balidan
Jago- Jago re Majdoor
Jago Jago re Kisan.

These songs used to leave remarkable impact on the Adivasis. He had helped a lot in taking Shibu Soren's movement to all the villages. When Shibu Soren started to spend more time in Santhal Pargana, Basant started to stay mostly in Gandey. He had also got connected to Jharkhand Mukti Morcha. There was no dearth of his opponents also. One day in 1979, when he was sleeping in his house in Gandey, some criminals killed him.

Jhagru Pandit

Jhagru Pandit was one of the most trustworthy associates of Shibu Soren. He is almost of the same age as that of Guruji. He lives in Karmatand block of Jamtara. He is considered to be a specialist in agriculture. When Shibu Soren had launched his 19-point programme, he had assigned the responsibility of agriculture to Jhagru Pandit. He used to stay with Shibu Soren. It was he who would decide where an embankment was to be erected, when and which crop was to be grown, how much fertiliser to be used, how much pesticides to be applied etc. Jhagru Pandit would advise the farmers about all this. He was with Guruji even during Chirudih incident. He had good knowledge of agriculture and he used to organise fairs also in his village. He was even honoured with many awards related to agriculture. How close he was with Guruji can be gauged from the fact that it was he who would show the works related to embankments and farming to the prominent journalists of the country whenever they visited Tundi to have a look at Guruji's accomplishments. Not only that,

Jgagru Pandit, Old Associate of the movement

when Shibu Soren had surrendered in front of DC, Dhanbad and had been sent to jail, Jhagru Pandit had forcibly accompanied him to jail.

Shyamlal Murmu

Shibu Soren treated Shyamlal Murmu like his younger brother. In fact, the Pokharia ashram was opened in Shyamlal Murmu's house. It was Shyamlal's mother only who used to prepare meals for Guruji. Shibu Soren used to have long hair those days. Many Adivasi youths had also grown long hair around the same time, just to confuse the police. Shyamlal Murmu and Sarkar Murmu were also among them. Many a time, the police were not able to make out who among them was the real Shibu Soren. Shyamlal used to play a vital role whenever Guruji conducted his court. He would be with Guruji like his shadow. When Guruji started to spend more of his time in Santhal Pargana after 1977, he had assigned the responsibility of his Pokharia ashram to this very Shyamlal. Shyamlal himself would conduct the court at the ashram. Later, there were also some complaints of favouritism against him. He was killed on 26 May 1994.

Rajendra Prasad Tiwari

Rejendra Tiwari, Education Minister in Shibu Soren's parallel government

Another important member of Shibu Soren's team was Rajendra Prasad Tiwari. He lived in Purnadih village of Tundi block. He was responsible for teaching Adivasis as part of Guruji's movement. He used to do this through Akil Akhara. Initially, he would himself bring children out of their homes to the school and teach them. Later, he took up an assignment as teacher in Nawadah.

Transformed Life Through Collective Farming, Night Schools and Animal Husbandry

As such, Shibu Soren had launched his movement in various regions including Gola, Petarwar, Jainamore, Bokaro and Dhanbad freeing the lands of Adivasis from the clutches of the moneylenders. However, it was the Tundi region where this movement attained maximum success. This was because Shibu Soren ran the movement in a planned way. He had succeeded in directly connecting thousands of Adivasis with the movement. The Tundi region was declared as a liberated area, which meant the area was controlled by Shibu Soren (Guruji) and not by the administration or the government. There was a major difference between Shibu Soren's movement and other movements. A movement for a separate Jharkhand state was already running in Jharkhand region for a long time but the same had not been as effective as the one run by Shibu Soren. He brought together people on a large scale. People did come to processions and rallies and participated in bandhs in earlier movements, but their impacts did not last long. On the other side, the movement run by Shibu Soren was providing immediate relief to the Adivasis. It was visible also. One, the lands that had been taken over by the moneylenders, either by deceit or by force, were getting restored. After many years, the Adivasis were able to get possession of the lands that belonged to them but had been snatched out of their hands. Restoration of a forcibly captured land to anybody helps in gaining trust in the movement not only of the person concerned but the entire village. The same thing happened with Shibu Soren's movement.

Guruji's movement was not limited only to restoration of lands. The real benefit of restoration of land or paddy cutting could be attained only when that land was subsequently used for farming or any other productive purpose. The attachment increased when the land could be used for, besides farming, some other purpose also that resulted in financial benefit to the owner. The same thing happened with Shibu Soren's movement. He defined his own model for village development. The Adivasis were trained for farming on the lands restored to them. For those who did not possess any land, arrangements were made for their participation in collective farming. Night schools were organised to make the Adivasis literate. Prohibition and animal husbandry were also given due importance.

Shibu Soren's 19-Point Programme

If the then Prime Minister Smt. Indira Gandhi had launched her 20-point programme, Shibu Soren was running his own 19-point programme in Tundi. He had launched his 19-point programme on 26 February 1975. These were the points.

Impart education through Akil Akhara to children as well as adults.

Collective farming (Rabi and Kharif compulsory).

Awareness among women through Women's Shilp Kala Kendra.

Library, Farmer's Library.

Collective Animal Farms (Hens, pigs, goats, cows etc.).

Hospital.

Plant conservation.

Gardening at all locations.

Fish farming in ponds.

Conservation of forest.

Road repairs.

Vigilance over rations.

Cottage Industry.

Ban on dowry for common good.

Ban on child marriage.

Minimum expenses on marriage ceremonies and reform in other social activities.

Reading rooms, music halls and theatres for entertainment.

Compulsory prohibition for common good.

Construction of Chetab Baisi and formation of Vichar Baisi at all locations for resolving disputes between Adivasis and non-Adivasis.

Shibu Soren had created a core team for implementation of above schemes. Prominent members of the team included Basant Pathak, Jhagru Pandit, Shyamlal Murmu, Kripal Singh and Rajendra Tiwari. Functions were assigned to each of them just like the portfolios in a cabinet. Shibu Soren was aware that the primary reasons for backwardness of the Adivasis were illiteracy, liquor and superstition. Those days, there was almost no literacy among the Adivasis. The region was also backward. There was poverty everywhere. Shibu Soren decided to make arrangement for education for all. They had to go to schools. Poor financial condition compelled even the children to work in farms during the day. Shibu Soren hence opened night schools to enable even the adults to get educated along with the children. This was called Akil Akhara. That region did not have electricity at that time. Initially, Shibu Soren made arrangements for lanterns from his own sources. Later, when he started working with the government, lanterns were procured out of government aids and donations from NGOs. Primary responsibility for children's education was assigned to Kripal Singh and Rajendra Tiwari. Kripal was the 'master sahib' of Akil Akhara. As per Shibu Soren's plan, every literate person was expected to teach at least five individuals. Each of those five in turn was expected to teach another five individuals. This campaign thus went ahead like a chain. Initially, the drive was limited to a few selected villages and later this got spread to other villages. Guruji thus laid a lot of emphasis on education in his own way; education was given importance in Pokharia ashram also and he himself used to teach. His efforts brought an awareness among the Adivasis towards education. It was his contribution towards education that prompted people to start calling him 'Guruji'. Even today, people call him Guruji out of their respect towards him.

Collective Farming

Shibu Soren knew that no change was going to take place till the time people were forced to live on empty stomach. They would pay attention to learning something only when they were not hungry. Hence, he took action on two fronts. First, he arranged training for the farmers to improve their farming for better production. He also taught them about other aspects like better quality seeds, better fertilisers and pesticides. By creating a system of irrigation through check dams across small rivers, he made

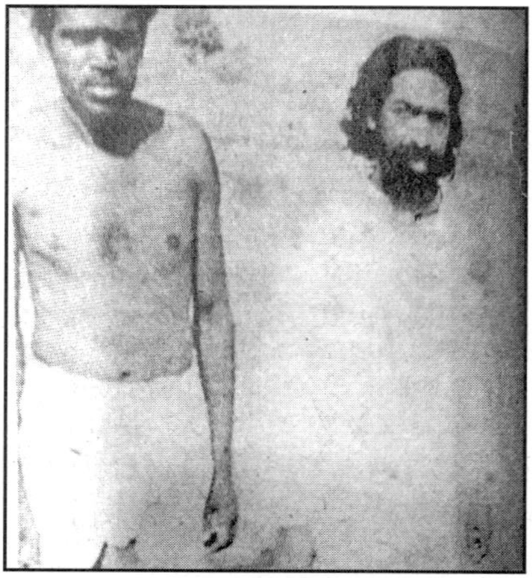

Jhagru Pandit and Shibu Soren during collective farming

it possible to grow two crops at the same place. Production of food grains got doubled. Check dams were built through voluntary work. Jhagru Pandit supervised all farming activities. He actually was the 'agriculture minister' of Shibu Soren. He was hence also called as 'Krishi Pandit'. Guruji also experimented community farming. Lands that were being recovered from the moneylenders used to be made available for community farming. The entire village would come together to grow crops on the same. Once the crop was harvested, the same used to be distributed among them based on the size of the land. One portion of the harvest used to be kept separate in the village for emergencies. For this, grain golas were built in all the villages. Any shortage in food grains in a village used to be filled by drawing grains from these golas. This experiment proved to be very successful. Guruji paid a lot of attention to prohibition also. Many of the villages were declared liquor-free. If anybody entered such a village drunk, he would get a good beating. Guruji and Basant Pathak used to monitor this personally.

Spend less on festivals (check this heading as animal husbandry also discussed)

Many of the schemes out of Guruji's 19-point programme had been implemented in a very effective way. Guruji wanted people to keep their expenses on marriages, parties and other festivals to a bare minimum; the money thus saved could be used for better education. For this, he had even suggested not celebrating festivals for long periods; traditions were to be definitely followed but wastage of time in the name of tradition was to be avoided. One of the campaigns of Guruji that was quite successful was animal husbandry. Hens, cows, pigs, goats etc. were distributed among the Adivasis. There was also a system of collective animal husbandry. One hen, one goat, one calf etc. would be collected from each house in the village and two youths from the same village would be assigned the job of taking care of them. This would also provide livelihood for two youths of the village. It was decided that one year later, those hens, goats and calves were to be returned to the original owners; only the originals were to be returned. The profits earned from these livestock were used for payment of wages to the youths, with the balance, if any, going to the common pool of village assets. The eggs laid by hens or kids born to the goats during that period of one year were treated as part of collective animal husbandry asset. Every house that contributed to this scheme benefitted to the extent that it received back the livestock properly grown over that period of one year - chicks as grown-up hens and kids as full-grown goats. Thus, Guruji had his own economic model.

A look at Shibu Soren's 19-point programme indicates how grounded he was. Attempts are being made today to put a stop to child marriages; Shibu Soren had made this a part of his campaign some fifty years back. He had implemented ban on child marriage. Many states have only now implemented prohibition whereas Shibu Soren had brought about prohibition in his operational area in the 70s itself.

Guruji conducted his own court

Earlier, the police used to handle all minor and major cases in Tundi and a large area around the same. The cases would go to courts and they would drag on for long periods. The common Adivasis had to spend money on the cases and they did not even get justice. Shibu Soren's movement had made such an impact that people had stopped going to police or courts for their issues. The entire region had been proclaimed by Shibu Soren as liberated area where he was running his parallel government. The Adivasis as well as other villagers had so much faith in Shibu Soren that they used to go to him to resolve their issues. He would conduct his own court and pronounce his judgement after hearing the parties. It was called 'Vichar Baisi'. The situation at that time was such that people used to take their cases to Shibu Soren's court instead of going to any police station or court. He had designated Pokharia ashram as the centre for this. He had even arbitrated hundreds of cases. Intellectuals, journalists and researchers from different parts of the country used to visit Tundi from time to time to understand the 'cut down paddy' campaign as well as other activities going on in the region. A social worker, writer and later professor in JNU Veer Bharat Talwar had spent some days in 1975 with Shibu Soren in his ashram. He had observed Shibu Soren's works while staying in the ashram. He had even made notes in his diary about the kinds of cases brought to Shibu Soren for arbitration. This is an authentic document.

Shibu Soren was there in Pokharia ashram on 1 August 1975. Four Muslims - Hakim Miyan, Siram Miyan, Hari Miyan and Raju Miyan from Machhawara village had come to him. They were requesting Shibu Soren with folded hands to permit them to carry on farming on some land. Their families were in trouble as the Adivasis had taken possession of their lands. In fact, their ancestors had come from other places and had settled in the village after conniving with the village chief. Later, they had slowly captured Adivasis' lands by force or got them transferred to themselves by deceit. Their houses gradually turned pucca while they continued to take over Adivasis' lands. The Adivasis were compelled to work as labourers on their own lands. When 'cut down paddy' campaign was launched, the Adivasis had forcibly harvested the crop from their lands. Their stand was that the lands belonged to their ancestors and they were dispossessed of the same by deceit. Hence, they were reclaiming their lands.

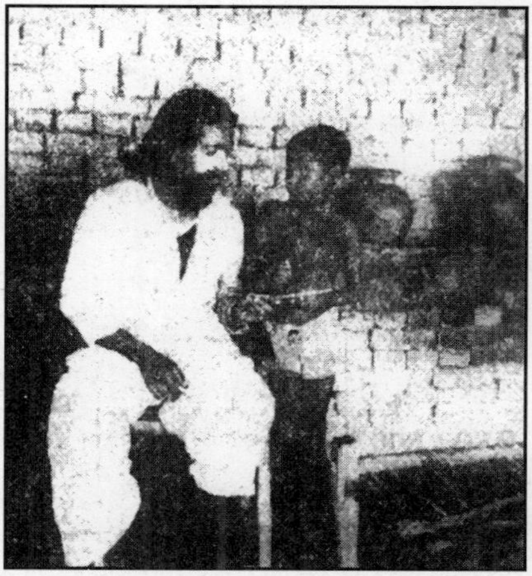

Guruji imparting treatment at Pokhariya Ashram

The impact of Shibu Soren's movement was getting visible. The Adivasis had started farming on those lands belonging to these four Muslims including Hakim Miyan. This was going on for the last two-three years. The situation had reversed. There was a time when moneylenders and landlords had control over the lands of the Adivasis and now those Adivasis had taken back their lands. This had made them starve for food.

Hakim Miyan, Siram Miyan, Hari Miyan and Raju Miyan had entreatingly pleaded before Shibu Soren, "We are in trouble.Our families are in trouble.We are now left with no land. We have been living together with you all for years. Where do we go now? Please restore some land back to us to enable us to cultivate the same and earn livelihood for our families." Shibu Soren had listened to them attentively. He then called a meeting of the villagers and pronounced his decision to include those four Muslims also in collective farming. They had to sow paddy together and decision with regard to distribution of grains was to be made later. Shibu Soren had taken that decision on humanitarian grounds.

However, the very next day, on 2 August, all the four Muslims came to Shibu Soren again and informed that the Adivasis had refused to permit them to cultivate land and had driven them away threatening that the lands belonged to their forefathers and they would not allow anybody else to cultivate the same. This created a grim situation, and indicated the level of hatred people had at that time against those who had exploited the Adivasis earlier. Such cases used to come up almost ona daily basis. In a few cases, the Adivasis did permit others to cultivate. This incident is also an evidence of the kind of changes the 'cut down paddy' movement had brought about; the Adivasis who had been yearning for years for possession of their lands had got their lands back. This was a real change.

The cases that were brought to the Vichar Baisi of the Santhals attracted court fees also. That was the rule. On 2 August, one more case related to land was brought to Shibu Soren. One Bhumihar, Chaudhary Singh from Shitalpur village, narrated his case like this - he had three acres of land; there were 18-20 members in his family; 25 dismils of land out of his land of one acre had been grabbed by Dheba Manjhi; the land earlier belonged to Dheba Manjhi; Dheba already had 22 acres of land. Chaudhary Singh deposited the court fee amounting to Rs 25.25 in Vichar Baisi and requested his case to be taken up for hearing. Vichar Baisi adjudicated permitting Chaudhary Singh to continue farming in the remaining 75 dismils in that 1-acre land. However, when it was time for sowing, he was prevented by the Adivasis to do the same. There was a time when Chaudhary Singh reigned supreme and he had forcibly taken over the Santhals' lands. The time had changed now. As he was not allowed to carry out sowing in his farm, he was entreatingly appealing for justice before Shibu Soren. It was not that Dheba did not have land. He already had 22 acres of land and

Vichar Baisi had already pronounced its decision permitting Chaudhary Singh to continue farming in the remaining 75 dismils of land. Dheba did not agree to abide by the decision, as he was not ready to allow anybody to take over the land that belonged his forefathers. Many similar cases used to come up where the hearings would go on for long. In many cases, problems were encountered even in implementing Shibu Soren's decisions.

Guruji's Works in Spotlight

The kind of constructive activities that Shibu Soren (Guruji) had been able to accomplish prompted prominent journalists of the country to visit Tundi region to learn about the same. The journalists personally observed the development model of Shibu Soren and published stories on the same in their newspapers and magazines. Among them, The Times of India, The Economic Times, Dinman and Blitz were the prominent ones. Jawaharlal Kaul of Dinman (who later became editor of Dinman) had personally visited Tundi and written in detail about Shibu Soren's works, including his personal experiences. All the cases against Shibu Soren had been withdrawn then. Impressed by his works, Indira Gandhi had extended help through the then Chief Minister Jagannath Mishra to give a push to Guruji's works.

When Jawaharlal Kaul had gone to Tundi to meet Shibu Soren, he was accompanied by Shyamlal Murmu, Police officer Kichingya and BDO Dasharath Prasad. It was not easy for them to locate Guruji. They had to go to Jadakhunti village for that. After traversing several villages, they found Guruji busy supervising construction of a barrage across a river in the midst of hills just beyond Jadakhunti. The barrage was being constructed through voluntary labour of the Adivasis. Jhagru Pandit was also present there. He knew where the barrage was to be built in order to retain water for the maximum period. During conversations, Jhagru had said, "The river has so much water that once the barrage is ready, this may provide irrigation for the entire year." One of the officials had remarked, "But the time for sowing wheat is now over." On hearing this, Jhagru Pandit, who was standing next to Shibu Soren, had responded immediately, "These people have read the books from America and Russia. We know the books of this soil only. Here, the weather is equally warm throughout the year and no frost occurs. Then, why can't we grow wheat at this time? I will change my name if I am not able to harvest the best produce here." Such was his self-confidence.

Later, Shibu Soren himself drove Jawaharlal Kaul on his motorcycle to all those locations where his works were in progress. They continued their conversation on the motorcycle. Guruji was proudly showing and describing everything to him. The track was hilly and driving a motorcycle on the same was not easy. However, Shibu Soren was comfortably driving his motorcycle. Suddenly they saw a crowd at a place. When asked, Shibu Soren explained, "The Adivasis are celebrating a festival. They waste most of their time in festivals. I have tried to convince them to spend less of their time and money on festivals. The time and money thus saved may be used for education of their children." At another location, some Muslims had approached them. They were upset, as they did not have a mosque nearby. Shibu Soren had told them that once the work on the barrage was over, the Adivasi youths would join them in building a mosque. Guruji had become popular in all the classes of the society and people used to come to him for resolution of all kinds of issues. This was the 'raj' of Guruji.

Scene After 44 Years

Jawaharlal Kaul had gone from Delhi to Tundi in 1976 to have a look at the works of Shibu Soren.

Fortyfour years after that, I managed to locate Kaul in Delhi and requested him to share his experiences. Kaul told me, "Whatever Shibu Soren might have been in government files those days, he was a messiah for his own people, his own Adivasi brothers. The situation gradually changed and he started feeling extra pressure from his family and the society. In such circumstances, a person usually gets caught up in some mess due to his weaknesses. Shibu Soren also had to go through the same. This happened as, under pressure, he had to later do something that he had been critical of during his movement." Kaul recollected many interesting facts. Kaul had asked Shibu Soren, "You are young. Youth Congress is in prominence currently. Why don't you join the Youth Congress?" Shibu Soren had replied, "People from Youth Congress had approached me. They even had made an offer. In response, I had made an offer to them (Youth Congress representative) to stay with me in Tundi for a week; had they stayed with me in this region for a week, I would have taken their offer and joined Youth Congress. However, after hearing this, they had left immediately and have not shown their face again."

Kaul had then (in 1976) asked Shibu Soren, "Are you a Marxist?" He had replied, "No. I have not read Marx. Whatever little I have read, I have read Gandhi and Jaiprakash only. I get inspiration from them." Shibu Soren's words had left a good impression on Kaul. As to Shibu Soren of today, Kaul said, "Everybody does begin well but later even take a wrong path and get caught up. The same thing happened with Shibu Soren also. His very simplicity is his symbol. Rao episode is an example of the same. Otherwise, who takes money and goes to deposit the same into a bank? Only an innocent person would do something like that. A cruel person can't do that. Politics requires both morality and pragmatism. Wherever there is politics, it is successful with pragmatism only. If there is mismatch between the two, politics would not be successful. The same thing happened with Gandhi and Jaiprakash also. Both of them had very strong moral characters, but they lacked pragmatism. Had Shibu Soren paid more attention to practical aspects, the situation would have been different. As such, his very simplicity and innocence are his assets."

Even journalists and groups of students from abroad used to come to observe and understand Shibu Soren's collective farming, night schools, court, animal husbandry etc. The famous journalist Darryl D'Monte also had come in 1979 from Mumbai. He had travelled from Dumka to Tundi along with Shibu Soren. He had even visited his Pokharia ashram. He had observed there how people used to come to Shibu Soren with their complaints. He had later written how Shibu Soren's movement was successful in eliminating the moneylending system and how he was awakening people towards education. He had been quite impressed. Shibu Soren had become quite popular as a social reformer on account of all such efforts. Shibu Soren had still not become a parliamentarian by then.

After a detailed research, A. R. Desai has given a description in his book 'Repression and Resistance in India' about Tundi movement led by Shibu Soren mentioning how Shibu Soren worked there and how even the moneylenders and landlords used to get punishments after hearing of complaints in the court of Shibu Soren. In fact, Shibu Soren's efforts had become famous in the entire country and people used to visit his place to look at his achievements.

The Police Officer, Who Became Guruji's Confidant

The conditions around Parasnath hills, Pirtand and Tundi were such that no government official or employee wanted to enter that region. Specially after the incident of murder of a Police inspector in Topchanchi, there was so much fear among the Police that if any police officer had to visit that region, he used to go there in plain clothes. Shibu Soren's movement was in full swing. He had already built his ashram in Pokharia by then. Though the ashram was located in Pokharia, he used to spend most of his time in villages located between Palma and Parasnath hills where he was also carrying out his social reform and development activities. It was almost impossible for the Police to enter those villages. Incidents of confrontations between Adivasis and moneylenders and landlords were being reported on a regular basis. The murder of the police inspector was a matter of concern for both the state and the central governments. Around that time only, the Bihar government had posted K. B. Saxena as the Deputy Commissioner of Dhanbad to bring the situation under control. Saxena had taken charge as the Deputy Commissioner on 5 August 1974. He had immediately called a meeting of the Superintendent of Police and other senior officers to assess the situation; many hard decisions also were taken in the same. They included action against the coal mafia also in addition to the agitators. Shibu Soren was in any case out of the reach of the Police; hence K. B. Saxena questioned A. K. Roy. Saxena wanted to collect reliable information on Shibu Soren as much as possible. He was formulating his strategy for the same.

The government was aware that it was not easy to catch Shibu Soren. His immense popularity was making even the administration hesitant to directly touch him. K. B. Saxena was sent as Deputy Commissioner with special instruction to somehow bring Shibu Soren's activities under control and arrest him. DC Saxena was collecting information about Shibu Soren from his own sources also and he was receiving some startling details. He was being informed that Shibu Soren was actually fighting for those Adivasis whose lands had been grabbed by moneylenders and that he was running a campaign for the eradication of evils prevalent in Adivasi communities and for their education. The information K. B. Saxena was receiving after reaching Dhanbad was just opposite to the details he had been provided earlier. DC Saxena hence changed his strategy. He wanted to meet Shibu Soren directly. For this, a contact person was required.

For this, there was need of a police officer or person who could win the trust of the Adivasis. Finally, one name came up - Bernad Kichingya. He was the police station incharge of Tundi at that time. The main reason behind his selection was that he belonged to an Adivasi community. He was also familiar with the region. Besides this, he also had the ability to handle the bitterness of the Adivasis and win their trust. Bernad later retired as DSP. When I was working on Shibu Soren's biography, I was looking for the police officer who had played a major role in his surrender. It was quite necessary to meet that police officer and get all details about the same. During Tundi movement, if there was any police officer that had the guts to meet Shibu Soren and talk to him without fear, he was Bernad Kichingya only. Both of them had full faith in each other and also understood each other better. Hence, it was necessary to find him. In the meantime, I came to know that he was currently in Ranchi. He had a relative named Anil Mahto. I have known Anil from the days of the movement. During 2013, I, along with Anil Mahto, had gone to meet Bernad Kichingya at his residence in Ranchi. Though he was not well at that time, he went on talking for hours. He had responded to my questions quite enthusiastically. It was clear from the talks how deeply he respected Guruji. I had tried to understand from him how did he manage to meet Shibu Soren for the first time and how did he persuadehim to meet the then Deputy Commissioner K. B. Saxena. What were the challenges then? He had provided many interesting details.

Tundi Police Station in-charge Bernad Kichingya who was the link between Shibu Soren and the Administration

Kichingya had said, "Though I was sent as the Station In-charge of Tundi in 1974 only, I had met

Shibu Soren earlier also. When I was posted as a junior inspector at Ramgarh in 1968, Shibu Soren had already launched his movement on a small-scale by then. Spreading from Ramgarh to Gola and Petarwar regions, the movement had reached Bokaro. Shibu Soren used to wear dhoti-kurta then and had a big moustache. I had met him 3-4 times but all those meetings had taken place many years back. We both had also met at the residence of Bennet Tirki (Baghwa) in Chitarpur. After that, I was transferred to Tandwa. During 1972, when Shibu Soren's movement was at its prime, I was transferred to Jogta station in Dhanbad. T. P. Sinha was the SP of Dhanbad at that time. He had been posted as SP in 1971 and continued there till June 1974. This was one of the toughest times for any police officer. When Adivasis had killed inspector Ghatak, I was the one who was sent to Tundi. I was worried that I might get caught in something terrible, but had to follow the orders anyway. The situation there was really bad. After that inspector's murder, no administrative officer or police officer would had come out of the headquarters alone. There was an atmosphere of fear everywhere. Especially, the moneylenders were more terrified. The condition was such that moneylenders used to tell their crying kids - keep quiet, else Shibu Soren would come! The entire forest and hilly region of Tundi and Parasnath was declared as liberated region and Shibu Soren reigned supreme there. Only his orders were followed. At his single call dugdugis would be beaten and, within no time, thousands of Adivasis would assemble together, ready with their traditional weapons.

"Neither Shibu Soren nor Adivasis of Tundi were responsible for the situation. The atmosphere of fear was created because of the moneylenders. I also was aware that Adivasis' lands were being forcibly grabbed. The Adivasis would be first entangled in debt traps and then, their lands would be grabbed on the pretext of the same. This was of course illegal. It was the moneylenders' terror before the movement. A non-Adivasi moneylender would first marry an Adivasi girl and then take over her land. After living together for some time, the Adivasi girl would be thrown out of the house by the moneylender. The poor helpless Adivasi girl would be then forced to labouring for her livelihood. Whenever any Adivasi took a loan, his lands, hens, goats, everything used to be held as pledge against the same. The principal amount would not come down and the interest would keep on accumulating. The moneylenders were all powerful. They even hired musclemen for recovery. If anybody had availed a loan and was not making repayments on time, the musclemen would take possession of grains lying in his house. Poor and helpless Adivasis were unable to do anything. They did get enraged by all these things but were just powerless.

"I was informed that a landlord named Pashupati Dah in Maira Nawatand was quite ruthless. He was expert in extending loans. He would even give loan forcibly to any person, just to trap him. And later, when the loan was not repaid, he would take over his land. He owned four trucks. Paddy crops lifted forcibly would be carried to markets using those very trucks. The situation was terrible. The moneylenders' hooligans would kidnap any girl who dared to venture out in the evening or in the night. Such incidents had already created lot of resentment among the Adivasis. Under such circumstances, I was posted as incharge of Tundi police station. I was assigned the responsibility to bring the situation under control and to somehow persuade Shibu Soren to join the mainstream. It was a difficult task for me, but I took the same as a challenge.

"I had heard the name of Shibu Soren, but I was not able to make out if this was the same Shibu Soren that I had met in Ramgarh six years back or somebody else. I wanted to meet Shibu Soren to confirm the same. I was confident that I would be able to win his trust once I meet him. Many of the officers had advised me against going out alone or entering forests there; but I was bent upon meeting Shibu Soren. I had the information that Shyamlal Murmu was one of his close confidants. I felt Shyamlal might help me in arranging meeting with Shibu Soren. Shyamlal lived in Pokharia. I met Shyamlal and requested him to arrange a meeting with Shibu Soren; he refused. After inspector Ghatak's incident, I did not want to take any risk.

Had I Not Shouted, I Would Have Been Killed

"I used to roam about alone in Tundi, just to get some information or come across a person that would take me to Shibu Soren's hideout. Meanwhile, I met one Koswa Tudu. I requested him to take me to Shibu Soren. He agreed and took me to a place where Shibu Soren was holding a meeting with around 150 Adivasis. The moment the Adivasis saw me from a distance, they got ready with their bows and arrows to attack me. Finding myself in danger, I shouted, 'I am unarmed. I don't have any arms. I have not come to catch anybody. I am myself an Adivasi and have come to meet Shibu Soren Ji.' I was fortunate that Shibu Soren himself heard me and he conveyed something to the armed

Adivasis. They all got back and waited for me to move ahead. Feeling afraid, I kept moving ahead slowly. Once I came near Shibu Soren, I introduced myself after formal salutations. I reminded him of our meetings in Ramgarh. We then shook hands and hugged each other. By then, the Adivasis present there had understood that I was a familiar person. Shibu Soren offered me a seat on his cot and asked the purpose of my visit. I apprised him of my posting as incharge of Tundi police station and told him that I would ensure that the atrocities that the Adivasis there had been suffering earlier were stopped. By that time, more than 200 cases had already been filed against Shibu Soren. In the first meeting itself, I tried to impress upon him the fact that he had so many cases against him and the police were already looking for him with an arrest warrant. How long could he hide in the forests? It would be better for him to get those cases closed slowly and fight against the exploitation openly as a popular leader. I told him, 'Impact will be visible soon as I have taken over charge here. No case against any Adivasi would be lodged so easily. They will get justice. I will do whatever is possible, but I need your support.'

"Shibu Soren also had got my signal. He needed some more time. Hence, he said, 'Let's meet again next Sunday; I will get some mutton cooked. We will have lunch together. We will discuss then.' In my first meeting with Shibu Soren, my entire focus was on winning his trust. I was also aware that even a single wrong step from my side would make it difficult for me to get away from there safely. I was just working on the plan to bring Shibu Soren into the mainstream; this responsibility was assigned to me by the district administration of Dhanbad. The following Sunday, I (Bernad, then Station In-charge) reached Shibu Soren's place as agreed. There was no fear this time, as Shibu's supporters were aware of our meeting. I didn't face any problem. I kept waiting at the place where I was called up to 2-3 O'clock. Nobody turned up. I for once felt that Shibu Soren might not be serious while calling me here again. But, suddenly after that, Shibu Soren arrived there on his motorcycle. People then started to gather around him. Cooking was done there itself and we also continued our conversation. That day, Shibu Soren asked me, 'You have power to grant bail, don't you? If you have, these people (Adivasi agitators) will go to your police station one by one and you go on granting bail to them.' I already had order from high command to be soft towards Shibu Soren and his supporters. Thus, process was initiated to grant bail at the police station itself to those Adivasis whom the police were looking for. The situation was changing. I started to grant bail in large numbers at the police station itself. The

Adivasis would come to the station and I would offer them a chair. Many a time, I would even offer tea to them and then release them on bail. I already had orders from above in this regard. SP Sahib had even given me Rs 1000 for this purpose. The word had gone all around that 'one of our own' had come as the station in-charge. The moneylenders went to the government complaining that the station in-charge was working hand in glove with Shibu Soren and he needed to be removed. However, the entire administration was standing behind me. After this incident, Shibu Soren and I came still closer. This was the first step towards bringing Shibu Soren into the mainstream. After this, I had personally apprised Saxena Sahib of all the developments. Later, Saxena Sahib had also gone to meet Shibu Soren at his place. He was, however, transferred after that. The new Deputy Commissioner had joined. He also reposed full confidence in me. I worked with him also. I was with him on that day also when Shibu Soren had surrendered. After surrender, he was in jail for a few days and later, once he was out, he took his campaign forward with support from the government. For me (for Bernad), this was a great achievement in my life."

How Did Shibu Soren Surrender?

Shibu Soren was running a parallel government in Tundi forests. An award was announced to catch him dead or alive. Dhanbad Police was under tremendous pressure from the government and the administration to arrest Shibu Soren. Did Shibu Soren surrender or did the Police arrest him during emergency period? This has been a matter of debate. If he did surrender, who was the Deputy Commissioner (DC) of Dhanbad at that time? K. B. Saxena or Laxman Shukla? Most of the people are even not aware of this! There was only one person who could, if at all, provide some authentic information in this regard. He was Jhagru Pandit - one of the oldest and most trusted associates of Guruji during his movement; trusted to the extent that he was with Shibu Soren when the latter surrendered. He even insisted and accompanied him to jail and stayed there together. Hence, it was necessary to get details about that Jhagru Pandit and get a first-hand account from him of their imprisonment and their life in jail.

Jhagru Pandit belongs to Hathbandha village of Karmatand near Jamtara. On 30 October 2013, I, along with my friend Vinay, had gone to meet him at his residence in Karmatand. He had narrated the entire story. Many of the moments while recalling the events and talking about Guruji had made him quite emotional to the extent that he could not stop tears in his eyes. We had to do a lot of consoling to calm him down. Jhagru Pandit had provided detailed accounts of all the events - right from his first encounter with Guruji to his surrender and subsequent days in jail. In his own words -

"In my village itself, I (Jhagru) used to come across news about Shibu Soren's movement and his activities. I was quite impressed by him. I was just aware that an Adivasi youth named Shibu Soren was fighting for restoration of lands to Adivasis in Tundi and nearby areas, and was also teaching them about farming and animal husbandry. I felt an urge to go and see him. During 1973-74, I first went to Dhanbad and then Tundi and I got a chance to meet Shibu Soren there. I told him, 'Why are you wasting your time here with Binod Babu and A. K. Roy? Come with me to Santhal Pargana.' Shibu Soren doubted me: 'Who is this man? Is he some moneylenders' agent making such a suggestion?' I spent a few days with Shibu Soren. I had seen how he was ceaselessly holding meetings, getting paddy crops cut from the lands of the moneylenders and ensuring restoration of lands to the Adivasis there. He was also running a campaign against liquor and *hariya*. He would not spare anybody who got drunk. He would punish him, that also in his own way. It was called 'Dilli Road'. He would say, 'This man has consumed liquor. Subject him to Dilli Road.' After that, the person who had consumed liquor would be asked to squat down. Shibu Soren would then put his hands on his shoulders and press down forcibly. This would make the person suffer 'thauns' (a local word) and the lower portion of his back would get abrasion. This very process was called 'Dilli Road'. The person would moan under pain and after making a promise not to drink again, would somehow manage to run away from there. It used to be interesting to watch all this.

"I returned to my village after meeting Shibu Soren. Though I had returned, my words had got embedded in his mind. He wanted to know everything about me. Hence, Shibu Soren (Guruji), accompanied by Parmeshwar Baske, arrived in my village one day. The police station in-charge Bernad Kichingya, who had become his confidant by then, was also accompanying him. A farming festival was in progress in the village. They first of all went there. Guruji bowed to pay respect to the paddy stored there. I had a fascination for agricultural activities. I even had good knowledge in farming. Hence, I was honoured with a gold medal in that festival. There itself I happened to meet Shibu Soren. He was in my village; hence I just took him to my residence on my motorcycle. My that very motorcycle was later burnt during the Chirudih incident. Shibu Soren looked at my house; he also visited my farm. He was quite impressed to see my farming. He told me, 'Next time when I come here, I would like to see your pucca house, not this raw house.'

"Those days, whenever Guruji made a long trip, he used to spend 1-2 days in a village itself. He had come to our village and here also, he stayed for a few days at my residence. He was a vegetarian; he used to take plain meals. He relished potato, green leaves, broad beans and kurthi daal very much. Arsa made with jaggery also was his favourite. Shibu Soren returned to Palma after a few days. After meeting Shibu Soren, I was also not able to focus on my work in the village. I wanted to work with him, participate in his movement. Hence, later I also went to him in Tundi. Shibu Soren had asked me to guide the villagers in farming activities. I stayed with Shibu Soren and many a time, in his company only, I used to get barrages built across streams with the help of Adivasi youths. This helped in storing water for irrigation.

"Let me now tell you about the administration, police and Shibu Soren. Many events took place in my presence. Many of them were violent also. There was disturbance all around. The government in fact wanted to kill Shibu Soren, but he was just beyond their reach. In the meantime, Saxena Sahib (K. B. Saxena) took over as Deputy Commissioner of Dhanbad. There was a police officer named Kichingya. He was an Adivasi and admired Guruji. Saxena Sahib had initially planned to take a hard line and arrest Shibu Soren. Later, he came to know that Shibu Soren was doing good work and that changed his mind. In the meantime, Kichingya had somehow managed to meet Shibu Soren, not once but many times, and had won his trust. The entire region was going through some change. Now, Shibu Soren's supporters were not being harassed; in fact, in many cases, bails were being granted at the level of police station itself. The anger among the Adivasi youths towards the police had come down considerably.

K. B. Saxena visited Palma alone

"One day, Saxena Sahib somehow managed to reach Shibu Soren, all alone (unarmed). Saxena

Sahib had been quite stubborn. He felt no fear, though hundreds of Adivasis armed with their bows and arrows were standing guard around Shibu Soren at that time. The reason was that Kichingya used to often talk about Saxena Sahib during his meetings with Shibu Soren. Shibu Soren was hence familiar with that name. That day, Saxena Sahib came to Shibu Soren and said, 'I am K. B. Saxena, new DC of Dhanbad. I have come just to meet you.' They hugged each other. This was a strange meeting. One was the DC and the other was a prominent agitator whom the police was searching. Both Saxena Sahib and Shibu Soren sat on the cot and had a long conversation. All those people standing around with bows and arrows were not able to make out why that man had come there.

"The conditions those days were such that even BDOs and COs did not have the courage to come to Shibu Soren's camp to meet him. However, Saxena Sahib reached there all alone. He was a different kind of person. He was a very honest officer, lean and thin but courageous. They both had some ripe jackfruit. Then, they had some mahua lattha (mahua cooked in ghee). Saxena Sahib said, 'Pack some lattha for me to take home also.' He had a different style of working. In the same meeting K. B. Saxena Sahib told Shibu

Soren, 'After observing you and talking to you, I feel you are in fact a messiah for the Adivasis and are fighting for the poor. But, you have adopted a wrong modus operandi for your fight; it is violent. It should not be like that. How long can you fight living in forests like this? Why don't you surrender before the law? You will get justice and then, you may continue the same struggle for the welfare of the same Adivasis in coordination with the government. The government will support you. It's ok if you don't want to do that. One day, fighting like this, you may even succumb to a police bullet. Hence, give a thought to what I am telling.' Saxena Sahib had conveyed his message in a very effective way. Shibu Soren was forced to think over the same. While leaving, Saxena Sahib said, 'Think about it seriously. I will come again someday. And whatever charges have been filed against you, I will try to get them withdrawn. This may take time also. But there will be some way out, that's what I hope.'

"After talking to his associates, Shibu Soren said, 'Ok. Take the same route that you used for coming here.'

"Next time, the Deputy Commissioner of Dhanbad K. B. Saxena came along with the Superintendent of Police and some other people also. There were some journalists also among them.

Shibu Soren had already been informed about their visit. However, his supporters were alert. 'Are the Police coming to arrest Shibu Soren?' - this thought had made them quite anxious. Hence, many of the Adivasi youths had positioned themselves on the trees lying on the route, ready with their bows and arrows.. They had been instructed to attack the police only when he was arrested, else they were to keep quiet. Saxena Sahib arrived. Nobody was arrested. On the contrary, a large meeting was held there, attended by almost 25 thousand Adivasis. Saxena Sahib himself also addressed the Adivasis. By that time, the Adivasis present there had understood that Saxena Sahib was a nice man and he was not going to create any problem. Rather, he was going to support them. Even in that meeting, Saxena Sahib referred to Shibu Soren as a messiah. A record of the meeting was created. The word spread all around that the DC had called Shibu Soren a messiah of the Adivasis. After this, the moneylenders came together. They opposed Deputy Commissioner Saxena. Whatever may be the reason, but immediately after this incident, Deputy Commissioner Saxena was transferred from Dhanbad. Even before being relieved, K. B. Saxena had sent a letter to the then Prime Minister Indira Gandhi through the chief minister of Bihar. In that letter, he had lauded the works undertaken by Shibu Soren. It was also suggested to somehow bring Shibu Soren into the mainstream; that might bring peace to the region and also open the possibility of utilising him in future.

"Before leaving after his transfer, K. B. Saxena was a little upset. He was disappointed that he was transferred even before ensuring the surrender of Shibu Soren. However, Saxena Sahib had in fact already created the ground for his surrender. Whatever persuasion he had to do, he had already done. In the meantime, Laxman Singh joined as the new Deputy Commissioner of Dhanbad in July 1975. Before leaving, Saxena Sahib had conveyed to the new DC, 'I have planted the sapling. Water it, help it grow and let it flower and bear fruit; make sure it does not get spoiled.' What he meant was that all the preparations for bringing Shibu Soren to right path were complete. Only compassionate persuasion could bring him to the right path; this had to be kept in mind. The new DC Laxman Shukla had spent time in Dhanbad earlier also. He ensured that the works done by Saxena Sahib were carried forward in a proper way and taken to the desired end."

Shibu Soren summoned to police station

Jhagru Pandit was narrating the story in a rhythm. He went on, "One day, the new DC

Laxman Shukla also went to Palma and met Shibu Soren. Kichingya also was accompanying him. He only used to be the link. The main purpose of this meeting was to convey to Shibu Soren that, though the DC had changed, the work initiated by Saxena Sahib would be continued and taken further ahead. In the meantime, Shibu Soren also had made up his mind: 'Things are in any case already in progress; it may be better to join the mainstream and take this very campaign further in a more intense way.' It was winter of 1975 (he could not recollect the date). I (Jhagru Pandit) was with Shibu Soren in Pokharia ashram. There were many other associates also there. That was when Kichingya (Tundi police station in-charge) came to the ashram and informed that DC Sahib was in the police station and he had called Shibu Soren there. There was a time when no government official had the courage to summon Shibu Soren; however, the relation had gradually developed to be so cordial that he was asked to come to the police station. Shibu Soren was told that a call would be arranged from the station itself for him to talk to Chief Minister Jagannath Mishra and some way out to resolve the issue would be discussed. Shibu Soren did not tell anybody about this at that time. After talking to Kichingya, he prepared to leave with him. Till that time, I was assuming everything to be normal, but when Shibu Soren, before leaving, handed over the key to the ashram and some documents to me, I suddenly had the feeling that there was definitely something odd. Why was he handing over the key? That certainly means something else. Kichingya and Shibu Soren left for the police station. Shyamlal and I also followed them to the police station. We found both the DC and the SP sitting there.

"Finding Shyamlal and me (Jhagru) at the police station, the DC asked, 'Why are you people here?' He then said that Shibu Soren might have to go to jail for a few days; that was required to set things in order. He assured nothing wrong would be allowed to happen there. The DC said, 'I am there for him. Gradually, all cases will be withdrawn; but that would happen through a legal process. For that, he will have to go to jail first.' I realised that Shibu Soren's surrender had been arranged in a proper way. An arrest would have resulted in sharp reaction; however, the situation was quite different when it was a question of surrender. Shibu Soren also had understood the situation and was ready for the same. The SP and the DC started to leave along with Shibu Soren in a car. I said, 'I also will go to jail.' The DC said, 'You don't have any case against you. How can you go to jail?' I responded, 'At least take me to Dhanbad.' The

DC agreed. We first went to the residence of DC Shukla Ji in Dhanbad. In the night, litti-chokha was prepared at his residence. We all had the same together. There only, the DC arranged a call to Chief Minister Jagannath Mishra. He assured, 'Every possible help will be extended. Efforts will be made to get the cases withdrawn. There is no need to get worried. You are with Shukla Ji (DC).' By that time, even Shibu Soren was feeling relieved. There was no sign of any anxiety on his face. We spent many hours at his residence.

"After the dinner was over, they started preparing to take Shibu Soren to jail the same night. I said, 'I will also go to jail.' The DC again said, 'You don't have any case against you. How can you go to jail?' People knew me by the name 'Krishi Pandit'. There was no case in the name of Jhagru. I immediately responded, 'The police may file a case instantly against anybody. Let me punch a police officer now; you may lodge a case and then send me also to jail along with Shibu Soren. When you can file 200 cases, what's the problem in creating one more case?' The DC agreed and took me also along with Shibu Soren to Dhanbad jail.

All facilities provided in jail

"Special arrangements had been made for us in jail. Not two or four but thirty-four blankets had been provided for our use. Shibu Soren was little worried after reaching jail. He told them, 'I am now in your shelter. Do whatever you want.' Neither of us could sleep the first night in jail. Next day early morning, DC Laxman Shukla came to us and enquired, 'Did you face any problem?' After talking to us for some time, he left. He sent six persons for massaging. A tailor came after some time. He took measurements for kurta-pyjama for Shibu Soren and kurta for me. We were provided milk in the evening. Milk was mixed with water. When DC Sahib came next time, he was informed of the same. DC Sahib said, 'Don't worry, I will make arrangements to send one and a half litre milk every day for you from my home.' We were also provided newspaper and radio. We started getting milk every day from his home. There were bedbugs in our cots. Shibu Soren said, 'Please get these cots removed and get the floor smeared with cow dung.' As per DC's instructions, two new cots were provided, replacing the old ones. It was winter season. We were also provided warm clothes. DC Laxman used to come every day and talk to us for some time. He took good care of us. One day, the DC asked, 'Would you like to have mutton?' Shibu Soren was a vegetarian. I however was non-vegetarian. Shibu Soren said, 'I don't eat meat;

please arrange the same for Jhagru.' They started cooking mutton every day for me after that.

Helped Geeta perform Chhath in jail

"People used to respect Shibu Soren a lot in jail. One day, a lady named 'Geeta' was singing a song. Shibu Soren asked me, 'Jhagru, what is this lady doing?' I replied, 'She is a Bihari woman and is lodged here in connection with some case. It's Chhath time. She performs Chhath every year; however, as she is in jail, she is not able to do the same this year. She is hence comforting herself by singing that song.' Shibu Soren immediately said, 'Tell her to go ahead with Chhath pooja. We will arrange for all the items required for her pooja.' After that, all the inmates in the jail observed fast for one evening and collected money to get items for her Chhath pooja. Those days, no arrangements used to be made for Chhath in jail; however, the arrangements were made only for Geeta. Even Geeta did not believe that Shibu Soren could make all those arrangements for her.

Visited Bokaro to talk to the Chief Minister

"We were spending days like this. All kinds of facilities were there. Even other inmates there were quite happy. Even their facilities had improved, as the DC himself used to visit every day. One day early morning, we both were woken up and told that we both had to go to Bokaro. The Chief Minister had come there. A face-to-face meeting was scheduled there. The gate of the jail was opened and we were taken to Bokaro in a car. Chief Minister Jagannath Mishra was already waiting for us there. We met him. He first talked to Shibu Soren separately and said, 'You people should now see the outside world also. The cases against you are getting withdrawn one by one. Arrangements have been made for the same. Bail will not be opposed by anybody from the administration. You will be free soon. Go and help us in the next election. You are doing great work for the Adivasis. Continue with the same. Even the police would not bother you. You will be provided all possible support from the government.' The Chief Minister later mentioned about providing Shibu Soren a jeep, a tractor, one hundred lanterns and many other items to enable him to carry on with his activities.

"Here in the jail, the news spread everywhere that Shibu Soren and Jhagru had been taken to some other place. The inmates went on strike. They were afraid of something wrong happening to us. By that time, Shibu Soren and I had returned from Bokaro. The inmates were relieved. We were set free after some days. Tractor, jeep, lanterns and all other things had already been provided. Shibu Soren did use them to take his work forward. Later, Shibu Soren and I one day went to meet the Chief Minister in Patna. After that, a meeting of Shibu Soren with Indira Gandhi was also arranged. She also had appreciated Shibu Soren's work. Shibu Soren also was quite happy."

Dr. Mishra Arranged Guruji's Meeting with Indira Gandhi

Dr. Jagannath Mishra was the Chief Minister of Bihar when Shibu Soren surrendered in 1975 on persuasion by the administration and the government. All this was part of strategy of the government. Those days, Shibu Soren had created terror to the extent that even police were not able to confront him. Hence, the then central government had asked for a report and advised the Bihar Government to take action against Shibu Soren. After getting to know the real situation, the then Deputy Commissioner K. B. Saxena had submitted a report which also included details of the good work done by Shibu Soren. When that report reached the prime minister, the entire strategy got altered. Indira Gandhi had understood that Shibu

Soren could be her major strength in future as Adivasis had absolute trust in him. Later, Indira Gandhi even had a meeting with him. In fact, Dr. Mishra had played a significant role in making Shibu Soren surrender and later arranging his meeting with the then Prime Minister Smt. Indira Gandhi. Dr. Mishra had taken over as Chief Minister of Bihar on 11 April 1975. Abdul Gafoor was the chief minister before him. That was the time when Shibu Soren was running his parallel government around Tundi. He had proclaimed Tundi as a liberated region. The police hesitated to enter that region. The police were looking for Shibu Soren. It was Abdul Gafoor only who had sent K. B. Saxena to Dhanbad as new Deputy Commissioner in order to control him. Saxena had succeeded in his efforts to take Shibu Soren into confidence. However, when Shibu Soren did surrender, neither K. B. Saxena was there as Deputy Commissioner nor Abdul Gafoor as Chief Minister. Both had been replaced. Dr. Mishra was now the Chief Minister and Laxman Shukla the new Deputy Commissioner.

Before he was sent to jail, a telephonic conversation between Shibu Soren and Chief Minister Dr. Mishra was arranged at the residence of the DC of Dhanbad. The meeting though took some time. When Shibu Soren was in jail after surrender, he was one day quietly taken out of the jail straight to Bokaro where his meeting with Dr. Mishra was arranged. That was a secret meeting that was not made public. Various stories relating to Shibu Soren's surrender had been in the news. Hence, I just thought - how about talking directly to the person who had been involved in the entire episode those days.

It was not easy to talk to Dr. Jagannath Mishra on this subject 42-43 years after the incident. During 2018, when Dr. Mishra was released on bail, Mithilesh had a long conversation with him on the entire incident at his residence in Patna. Dr. Mishra had narrated the entire story and had been quite indiscreet. The story even includes some details that are being made public for the first time. It was surprising to note that Dr. Mishra remembered the entire incident and had narrated the full story without stopping. Just a few months after this interview, Dr. Mishra had left for his heavenly abode. During this conversation, Dr. Mishra had accepted that at his instance, Shibu Soren was brought out of jail for a talk with him at Bokaro and he had persuaded him to see the outside world. Here is the entire story about Shibu Soren's surrender in the words of Dr. Jagannath Mishra -

"The then Bihar government was not at all serious towards the problems of Jharkhand province. Though Ranchi was the sub-capital of Bihar officially, nobody was paying any attention to its basic problems. Exploitation of the Adivasis, dispossessing them of their lands and their migration were the fundamental problems of the region. Besides this, there was another major problem - usury.

"Usury was a major issue in the region; however, none of the governments sitting in Patna, the capital of Bihar, took any steps to get the same properly looked into. Nobody bothered to think how the rights of the Adivasis could be secured, how they could be made entitled to their share in the prices of the forest produce. The Adivasis regarded forests as their own territory and hence, they felt it was their right to get a share of the income generated by sale of forest produce of the region. They were not receiving that share and this had created a lot of resentment among them.

"These issues were first raised during the time of Birsa Munda and later by Jaipal Singh Munda. In order to control his movement, Binodanand Jha offered inducements to the Jharkhand Party. Jaipal Singh Munda was made a minister. This step of the government helped in bringing down the intensity of the movement of the Adivasis and their bitterness to a great extent. When I (Dr. Jagannath Mishra) took over as the chief minister of Bihar, I found that there was a law that prohibited any sale of Adivasis' lands. Non-Adivasis were not allowed to buy Adivasis' lands. Despite that, the Adivasis were being dispossessed of their own lands on a large scale. I made arrangements for restoration of their lands. The Adivasis were being dispossessed of their lands, as they were not aware of the law.

"I created a Mobile Magisterial Team to eradicate this problem. This team could go to various villages and register complaints. Around that time only, Shibu Soren emerged as a social-reformer in the region. Shibu Soren was educating the Adivasis against drinking. He was sensitising the Adivasis against drinking *hariya*. However, his movement was violent and that's the reason quite a number of cases had been lodged against him.

"He would use violent means to snatch lands from non-Adivasis and restore them to the Adivasis. We launched efforts to bring the Adivasis to the mainstream. Chhotanagpur Santhal Pargana Development Authority had already been created before I assumed power. It had its headquarters located in Audrey House, Ranchi. The secretariat was set up in Audrey House. It was empowered to grant approvals at Ranchi itself for the schemes that were earlier sent to Patna for approval. However, this authority was facing a lot of operational problems. This secretariat was not able to function properly because of Shibu Soren's violent movement.

"We split the authority into three parts - Santhal Pargana, North Chhotanagpur and South Chhotanagpur. We also put in place a mechanism to implement all the schemes in Jharkhand region through these authorities only. No proposal was required to be sent to Patna for approval. Despite all these efforts, the exploitation of the Adivasis did not stop. The then Prime Minister Indira Gandhi also, during her regime, had made attempts to resolve this issue in her own way. There were several cases registered against Shibu Soren. He would run his movement clandestinely, but used to organise a large gathering every year in February. I decided to have a meeting with him. I took Prime Minister Indira Gandhi into confidence for the same. We had a meeting at Bokaro with the mediation of Laxman Shukla, then Deputy Commissioner (DC) of Dhanbad. It was a secret meeting. I gave an assurance to Shibu Soren that all the cases against him would be withdrawn if he came back to the mainstream. After this meeting, he agreed. We provided him with a tractor and other farming implements to enable him to carry on farming and also help others. With the consent of Indira Gandhi, I took Shibu Soren to Delhi and arranged his meeting with the prime minister. At the instance of Indira Gandhi, a tractor was provided to Shibu Soren. Indira Gandhi counselled him to use the same for common good, for helping and serving people.

"We returned after that meeting. Sometime after that, it was time for 1980 elections. We were looking for strength. After discussing with Indira Gandhi, we entered into an agreement with Shibu Soren. Congress allotted 19 seats to Shibu Soren's party. However, this alliance between Congress and Shibu Soren did not last long. It was broken very soon. The primary reason for the same was that Congress had started feeling that I (Jagannath Mishra) would have personally become stronger with that. Though Congress had broken alliance with Shibu Soren, I had played my part in bringing him to the mainstream. I was successful in making a fugitive return to the mainstream. I had several meetings with Shibu Soren. All the meetings were secret, but whatever happened next was a public event. Shibu Soren's surrender was a major political event at that time. I was not in favour of creation of a separate Jharkhand state. I wanted one-third out of all the investments in Bihar to be made in Jharkhand province to ensure development of the region to a desired level. For this, all the powers and discretions that were used for taking decisions in Patna were vested to the three development authorities at the secretariat at Ranchi.

"The truth is that I never had any meeting with Shibu Soren at the Circuit House. He hesitated to go there. He used to meet me at some private places only. He was too hesitant to go to official locations. Whenever I visited Jharkhand region, he would definitely come to see me. He and his entire family had a lot of respect for me. I am not meeting Shibu Soren now.

"Let me tell you one more thing. I had persuaded Shibu Soren to end his movement. Work had already been initiated on the programme that I had put together for the same. Setting up of the secretariat at Ranchi, vesting of powers to the three development authorities and change in their working style - all these steps had made the Adivasi community and their leaders quite satisfied. Hence, the demand for a separate state had lost steam. I had cajoled Shibu Soren into abandoning his demand for a separate Jharkhand state. He was in fact ready for the same; however, people provoked him later, especially the Bharatiya Janata Party fanned Shibu Soren's demand. Basically, it was BJP that breathed new life into the demand for a separate state; else, the issue had already met its end.

"None of the committees of the Bihar government ever recommended constitution of a separate Jharkhand state. I (Dr. Jagannath Mishra) had even asked BJP leaders why they were in favour of dividing Bihar into two parts when I (Dr Mishra) had already resolved the issues of the Adivasis; why they were fanning the demand for a separate Jharkhand state when the movement for the same was almost dead. Many of the Bharatiya Janata Party legislators had been elected from Jharkhand region and hence, they believed that they would be benefitted by creation of a separate state; that's why they did so.

"Now, along with Shibu Soren, let's talk a little about Suraj Mandal also. Suraj Mandal played a major role in defaming Shibu Soren. Suraj Mandal also had a role in leading Shibu to a wrong path. He only was involved in the cash deal with Narasimha Rao. Shibu Soren had not accepted the cash directly. It was Suraj Mandal who did everything. He spoiled Shibu Soren; else Shibu Soren was just running his social movement. His movement was, though, violent. Hence, multiple cases were getting registered against him one by one. After we met and he surrendered, all the cases registered against him were withdrawn."

Minister Attends Guruji's Meeting in Palma

Shibu Soren did not keep quiet after he was released from jail where he was sent subsequent to his surrender before Dhanbad district administration during emergency period. He took his campaign forward just the way he used to do earlier. There was, though, a difference - earlier, he had many cases registered against him, now all the cases were withdrawn. This was helping him. The Bihar government and Shibu Soren himself wanted to convey the message that everything had come to normal, Shibu Soren had joined the mainstream and the government was extending all possible help to the Adivasis.

Chief Minister Dr. Jagannath Mishra had himself taken on the responsibility of getting Shibu Soren released from jail and getting the cases against him withdrawn. Dr. Mishra was constantly taking directions in the matter from

Prime Minister Indira Gandhi. The deputy commissioners of the districts where Shibu Soren's movement was running and where cases were registered against him were also regularly getting communications from the government in this regard. Dhanbad was of course a different case. Laxman Shukla, Deputy Commissioner of Dhanbad was in fact the anchorman of the efforts for bringing Guruji out of the forests. He had just taken the work of K. B. Saxena forward. Congress as well as the government wanted to utilise Guruji to maximum extent. All efforts were being made to ensure constant improvement in Guruji's relationship with Congress. Immediately after Guruji's surrender, an audiotape containing his appeal for peace was prepared and the same was replayed in all the villages in Dhanbad region.

It was now the turn to organise a large gathering. Arrangements were made for Chief Minister Dr. Jagannath Mishra and Shibu Soren to share the stage in this first gathering; however, for some reasons, he could not come. Shibu Soren's first meeting was held in Palma on 27 February 1976 in the presence of a minister of Bihar government. The then Education Minster of Bihar Dr. Ramraj Singh had participated in that meeting. Shibu Soren was there on the stage and he had addressed the massive gathering of the Adivasis. L. K. Jha, a

First time after surrender, Shibu Soren (in dhoti-kurta) sitting on the stage in a meeting organised at Palma

lawyer in Dhanbad, had chaired the meeting. The meeting was meant to convey the message that the government would henceforth support Shibu Soren in his efforts and all the schemes that he had been running for the Adivasis would be further speeded up. Shibu Soren himself lauded the efforts of all - right from the chief minister to the government and the district administration. Shibu Soren and the Education Minister sharing the same stage was the main attraction of the meeting. Nobody had even imagined this, six months ago. Before this, the government had announced an award for killing the same Shibu Soren. The police were looking for him. It was the same region, especially

Palma, of Shibu Soren, where no government officer or police officer dared to enter without his permission. Today, a minister was attending a meeting in the same Palma without any fear. Over 50000 Adivasis were present there to listen to his speech. This was the change.

Shibu Soren (Guruji), in his dhoti-kurta, was present on the stage. From the same stage, Shibu Soren, speaking to the audience, had claimed that nobody else but he could do good to the Adivasis and the Harijans. There was no doubt that the government had launched an umpteen number of schemes for their upliftment. Individuals from Adivasis and Harijans were appointed as officers, but that did not result into any major benefit, as they did have some demerits. Drinking was the biggest obstacle in their development. Shibu Soren had appealed to the Adivasis to beware of the selfish elements that wanted to use them as their baits for serving their own interests.

At that time, Congress used to oppose the demand for a separate Jharkhand state. By then, Jharkhand Mukti Morcha had already been formed; however, the main priorities for Guruji were the elimination of moneylending system and upliftment of the Adivasi community. His close contacts with Congress had also resulted in greater impact of the government on him. This became visible when Shibu Soren was delivering his speech at Palma. Referring to the demand for a separate Jharkhand state, he had said, "Where is the need for the same? We are already living in Jharkhand region. The need of the hour is to uplift and develop the living conditions of the simple and poor Adivasis and non-Adivasis inhabiting the region." Shibu Soren had further said, "Our efforts would be successful only by properly implementing the measures taken by our popular Chief Minister of Bihar Dr. Jagannath Mishra." Repeating his earlier announcement, he had said that they were committed to make the 20-point programme announced by the Prime Minister (Smt. Indira Gandhi) successful. Shibu Soren had said, "If every district administration behaves like Dhanbad administration, there would be no problem for the Adivasis or non-Adivasis in those regions. The Deputy Commissioner (Laxman Shukla) of this district (Dhanbad) has taken a lot of interest, treating it to be his own work, in implementing the schemes launched by the government for the Adivasis and the Harijans. He has tried to resolve all local issues treating them to be his personal issues. That is the reason that though there was expectation of large-scale violence during paddy cutting, not a single instance of even a minor scuffle has been reported. Thousands of Adivasis and non-Adivasis living in the region now look up to the deputy commissioner with belief and trust." This speech by Shibu Soren had made it clear that he would henceforth work in coordination with the district administration and the state government would also support him in his efforts.

Shibu Soren in a meeting with administrative officers

When the chief guest Education Minister Dr. Ramraj Singh came to the stage in Palma from where Shibu Soren had also delivered his speech, he made the announcement for opening of primary and secondary school in every Adivasi village. He also announced the proposal for opening a state-sponsored high school for poor Harijan and Adivasi children. The Education Minister said, "The night schools that Shibu Soren is running in this region would be provided government aid." The Education Minister had openly praised Shibu Soren and had remarked that he had never seen, anywhere in the entire country, such a silent campaign for social reform and economic upliftment. He said that the good work that Shibu Soren was carrying on in Tundi region appeared very much to be a part of the 20-point programme.

After this meeting at Palma, the administration and the state government also engaged Shibu Soren for promoting Prime Minister Indira Gandhi's 20-point programme. Shibu Soren had already promised to launch the campaign for implementing the 20-point programme. And he actually did that. He had taken part in the Dhanbad district administration's event and appealed people for making the 20-point programme a success. He used to be invited to such events. Besides Dhanbad, events were organised for Shibu Soren in various regions of Santhal Pargana also. Shibu Soren enjoyed doing this, as there was not much of difference between Prime Minister's 20-point programme and his (Shibu Soren's) own programme. Hence, Guruji felt that he was in fact promoting his own programme and not that of the government.

Santhal Pargana as New Hub

Shibu Soren had started visiting some areas of Santhal Pargana much before the days when he was running his parallel government in Tundi and Parasnath forests. Most of those areas were located close to Tundi. The Jharkhand Mukti Morcha was yet to be formed. Shibu Soren (Guruji) also wanted to visit Bhognadih, the pious land of Sido-Kanhu. Around that time, Guruji was introduced to Digambar Marandi who originally belonged to Ramgarh in Dumka. Marandi was then a student of a college in Dhanbad and he used to hear stories about Guruji's struggle. This relates to the year 1970. Marandi had later taken up a government job and hence, he did not use his full name just to hide his true identity. He was known as 'D. Marandi' those days. He was connected to the movement also. There was a risk of losing his job if his real name got revealed.

Guruji had gone to Bhognadih for the first time in 1972, accompanied by D. Marandi and Nandlal Soren. There was no plan for any campaign or meeting. He had gone there just to see the place and pay homage to the pious land of Sido-Kanhu. Guruji had heard the stories of bravery of Sido-Kanhu and that was the main reason he wanted to visit the place. And he did visit. Even after that, Guruji continued to make trips to this area. By that time, Jhagru Pandit of Karmatand in Jamtara had already come in contact with Guruji. He was even staying with Jhagru Pandit. In the meantime, the Adivasis of Santhal Pargana also had come to know that Shibu Soren was fighting against the moneylenders and was even getting lands restored. Hence, the Adivasis in different areas in that region had started making demands to invite Guruji. Guruji also had started making visits to those areas intermittently.

The Chirudih incident occurred in the meantime. It was 22 January 1975 when Guruji had gone to Jamtara crossing Pabia for a meeting. On his way back, some moneylenders and CPI workers attacked Shibu Soren by blocking the road very close to Pabia. Shibu Soren somehow managed to escape but the attackers got hold of Jhagru Pandit and assaulted him badly. They even set his motorcycle on fire. The situation was such that they would have possibly killed Shibu Soren had they caught him. Shibu Soren only was their target. The moneylenders had made a complete plan for his murder. When the Adivasis came to know about the attack, it made their blood boil for a revenge. Next day i.e., 23 January 1975, thousands of Adivasis armed with their bows and arrows and other traditional weapons stormed Chirudih village and killed 11 moneylenders and their supporters. Shibu Soren's name quickly got widely known in Santhal Pargana after this incident.

Shibu Soren controlling the crowd with a ruler in his hand during a meeting in Santhal Pargana in the 70s

On 13 March 1976, the first meeting of Shibu Soren in Dumka was organised in Jaherthan near Santhal Pargana College. The students in the hostels had then welcomed him. Guruji had in fact spent his night in Champa Hostel there. The meeting was attended by just 70 to 80 persons, including Simon Marandi, Masi Soren, Sate Hembram, Chadra Murmu, Father Anthony and Dubraj Tudu. The meeting had run for the entire night. During that trip, Shibu had visited Champa Hostel as well as Shibu Murmu's house in Gidhani. Shibu Soren had planned to return to Chatra that day. Sate Hembram had then sent for the jeep belonging to the owner of Gyanada Talkies to take him to Chitara to meet Narsimha Murmu and then return to Dhanbad. Shibu Soren's support base in Dumka got a fillip after this meeting. He started to attend programmes in Santhal Pargana also. In fact, after Shibu Soren was released from jail subsequent to his surrender, he was being utilised for dissemination of information on the 20-point programme. Many of the social initiatives that Guruji had undertaken in Tundi matched with the items covered under Prime Minister's 20-point programme. Hence, a written communication used to be sent whenever Shibu Soren's programme was scheduled in any village.

A notice was issued by D. Marandi on 1 March 1976 from Tundi. It read like this - 'An energetic leader of Jharkhand Mukti Morcha Shri Shibu Soren is coming to Dumka on Saturday, 13 March 1976 to meet all Adivasi leaders and social workers of Santhal Pargana for promoting social upliftment efforts and 20-point programme. Hence, you are requested to reach Dumka on the date mentioned above to meet him.' This notice proves that Shibu Soren had started to meet people openly everywhere after January 1976. This was because all the cases against him had been withdrawn and he did not have any fear of arrest. He was now freely carrying on with his 'cut down paddy' campaign in Santhal Pargana. The lands of the Adivasis that the moneylenders had grabbed forcibly, he started to get them freed the same way that he used around Tundi.

Shibu Soren was introduced to Suraj Mandal in 1976 only. Mandal was earlier in Youth Congress and was considered a strong pillar in Santhal Pargana. When Shibu Soren started frequenting Santhal Pargana and his impact was visible all around, Suraj Mandal also got influenced by him. Later, Suraj joined him in the Jharkhand Mukti Morcha. Mandal's entry started inducing non-Adivasis also to lean towards JMM.

Very soon, the 1977 assembly election was round the corner. Shibu Soren contested the election from Tundi assembly constituency; however, despite his popularity, he lost the election to Satya Narayan Dudhani. After this, Shibu Soren decided to make Santhal Pargana his base for future political activities. After the 1977 election, Shibu Soren used to spend most of his time in Santhal Pargana. All across Santhal Pargana, he launched his movement, similar to the one he earlier ran in Tundi region against moneylenders, landlords and exploiters. The support he received in Santhal Pargana was still better. A large portion of Santhal Pargana is hilly and it was not easy even for the police to enter those regions and take any action.

Shibu Soren Arrested Under Karpoori Government

While Shibu Soren lost his assembly election from Tundi, Simon Marandi won the Littipara assembly seat as an independent candidate. Guruji had influence on Simon Marandi. Simon had participated in some of Guruji's programmes even before becoming a legislator. Simon Marandi also joined Shibu Soren in 1978. Shibu Soren's strength kept on growing. In December 1978, when it was time to harvest paddy, Shibu Soren, Suraj

Mandal and their supporters intensified their 'cut down paddy' movement. Guruji's supporters started to forcibly harvest crops in the tribal lands taken over by the moneylenders. This led to fierce encounters with the police and the moneylenders. It was the government of Karpoori Thakur in Bihar at that time. The speed with which this movement spread across Santhal Pargana scared the Bihar government. Shibu Soren and Suraj Mandal were arrested. Both of them were sent to Bhagalpur jail. The government was expecting the 'cut down paddy' movement to die down after arrests of Shibu Soren and Suraj Mandal; but it did not happen. More than one lakh Adivasis gathered on roads in Dumka in protest of the arrests. They were armed with their traditional weapons. They blocked the roads. The entire Dumka town was subjected to 'ghera dalo-dera dalo' campaign. This had a huge impact on the government. The government had never even thought that Shibu Soren's arrest would result in such a massive reaction and that people in such large numbers would throng the roads. Chief Minister Karpoori Thakur deputed his Finance Minister Kailash Pati Mishra to Dumka to assess the situation. On receipt of his report, the government, in a bid to pacify the situation, issued orders to release Shibu Soren and Suraj Mandal. After 40 days in jail, Shibu Soren came out of the jail in January 1979 and the situation returned to normal. The Bihar government breathed a sigh of relief.

Karpoori Thakur personally attends JMM meet

Karpoori Thakur had realised Shibu Soren's strength; hence, he in a way adopted a path of conciliation. A large meeting was organised after Shibu Soren's release. Chief Minister Karpoori Thakur himself came to Dumka to attend the meeting. He addressed the meeting. In his speech, he said, "I salute my Adivasi brothers and sisters. We will together develop Bihar. I do not wish to see you all separate from Bihar." Karpoori Thakur was amazed to see the crowd at Shibu Soren's meeting. People from far-off places, with food packs on their back, had come barefoot to attend the meeting.

Dumka: When He Became Parliamentarian For the First Time in 1980

Right when Shibu Soren had launched his struggle against moneylenders, he had decided to initiate social reform campaigns also; however, if required, he was ready to even contest elections and enter politics. And he did the same. He had set this in motion in the 70s itself from Barlanga. Election for the position of Mukhiya for Barlanga Panchayat was being conducted then. He decided to contest that election. That was the beginning of his struggle. He was just getting popular. This was the first election for Shibu Soren. He lacked experience and was not aware of political machinations. The moneylenders joined forces and managed to defeat him in the election with a low margin; however, Shibu Soren did not lose heart even after this loss. He gradually improved his contacts with leaders of political parties. During 1968-69, Shibu Soren stayed with Mazharul Hasan Khan, a leader belonging to Communist Party of India, and also learned politics. Mazharul Hasan Khan was quite popular around Ramgarh. He had contested 1969 Assembly election from Ramgarh and had lost; but he had contested the next election i.e., 1972 election from both Ramgarh and Jaridih constituencies. He had won the Ramgarh seat but lost Jaridih. It was unfortunate that soon after winning the election, he was murdered in MLA quarters in Patna. Guruji had later separated from the BJP and had joined Bagun Sumbrui's All India Jharkhand Party for some time. He had even organised a meeting for Bagun Sumbrui at Bokaro in the year 1970.

First Assembly Election

It was in 1972 when Shibu Soren had contested for an Assembly seat for the first time. He did not have the name 'Shibu Soren' then. People knew him by the name 'Shivcharan Manjhi'. It was Jaridih assembly constituency. This relates to the year 1972. Jaridih used to be an assembly constituency at that time. Shibu Soren had become popular on account of his continuous fight against moneylenders. He was running the Adivasi Sudhar Samiti in Jainamore. He had taken the decision to contest election on the

Shibu Soren taking oath as a Central Minister

suggestion of his supporters. The last election in Jaridih was held in 1969 when Shashank Manjari belonging to the House of Ramgarh had won; however, she was not there to oppose Shibu Soren in 1972 election. He had the backing of Kolhan Adivasi leader Bagun Sumbrui on account of his movement. Bagun Babu was then considered a prominent leader of Jharkhand Party, as he along with N. E. Horo and Devendra Manjhi had kept Jharkhand Party alive after Jaipal Singh had switched to Congress. Shibu Soren had contested that election under the banner of Jharkhand Party. In this election, Shibu Soren (Shivcharan Manjhi) had contested against Bharatiya Janata Party leader Chhatru Mahto. Shibu Soren had secured fourth position with 4984 votes only. Chhatru Mahto from Jan Sangh had won the election with a margin of around 200 votes. This loss did not discourage Shibu Soren. In the meantime, his area of operations had also expanded and he was spending most of his time around Tundi. He enjoyed immense popularity there.

Year 1977: Contested Assembly Election from Tundi

The next election was held in 1977. The conditions had changed after emergency. Shibu Soren had undergone a significant transformation during the period from 1972 to 1977. After 1972, Shibu Soren had launched a massive movement in Dhanbad-Giridih and dozens of cases had been registered against him. He had been established as a prominent leader of the Adivasis. He had even formed the Jharkhand Mukti Morcha with support from Binod Bihari Mahto and A. K. Roy. He had surrendered in the middle of the emergency and had even gone to jail. He was later released. For most of the cases against him, either the charges were withdrawn or he was granted bail. Hence, he did not have any issue in contesting 1977 assembly elections. The 1977 elections were being held after emergency. Janata Party had already been formed. Shibu Soren had decided to contest the election from Tundi constituency. He did contest, as an independent candidate. JMM was yet to be registered then and hence, despite the formation of JMM, its candidates had to contest the election as independent candidates. He was facing Satya Narayan Dudhani of Janata Party. In that election, another leader of Jharkhand Mukti Morcha Shakti Nath Mahto was also in the field as an independent candidate. Both Shibu Soren and Shakti Nath Mahto had the same vote bank. Hence, there was a danger of votes getting split between the two. And that is what happened. Not only Shakti Nath Mahto but Shibu Soren also lost the election. Satya Narayan Dudhani was the winner. Shibu Soren lost and was placed at second position. This election even resulted in some estrangement between Shibu Soren and Binod Babu. Shibu Soren felt that Shakti Mahto was fielded from the same constituency where he was contesting just to make him lose.

First Time Parliamentarian from Dumka in 1980

Loss in 1977 Tundi assembly election forced Shibu Soren to contemplate whether he required to continue with his area of operation around Tundi or shift somewhere else. Tundi had a good population of Adivasis. Shibu Soren had fought a long battle there against moneylenders. He was popular also. He was unable to determine the reason for his defeat there despite all this. Finally, he decided to look for a new territory. In the course of his movement, he used to make trips from Tundi to Santhal Pargana on a regular basis. Shibu Soren's old associates Digambar Marandi, Jhagru Pandit and Simon Marandi advised him to make Santhal Pargana his new centre and contest the next election from there only. In the meantime, Chaudhary Charan Singh's government in the centre fell after the withdrawal of support by Congress. Mid-term poll for the parliament was declared. This happened in the year 1980. Shibu Soren decided to contest the parliament election from Dumka. This was the first time that Shibu Soren was contesting a parliamentary election. Even before this election, Shibu Soren had developed good relations with Congress. This had happened on the initiative of Gyan Ranjan. However, no understanding could be reached with Congress for this parliamentary election. Shibu Soren contested the 1980 election as an independent candidate. He was being challenged by Bateshwar Hembram who had won the same seat in 1977; Hembram was a candidate of Janata Party. Besides him, Prithvi Chandra Kiskoo from

Congress was also in the field. Despite all this, Shibu Soren succeeded in winning the election by 3,513 votes. He became a parliamentarian for the first time. Prithvi Chandra Kiskoo was at second position. This was a major achievement for Shibu Soren, as he was the first leader from Jharkhand Mukti Morcha to become a parliamentarian. It's a different matter that he had secured this win as an independent candidate. The Election Commission had not allotted a separate election symbol to his party till that time.

Year 1984: Lost from Dumka under Sympathy Wave

By winning the 1980 election from Dumka, Shibu Soren had proved that his decision to contest parliamentary election from Dumka was correct. Shibu Soren's stature suddenly got a boost with this win. Before that, he was known only as a militant leader of Jharkhand. Very soon, it was time for 1984 elections. During this term of 1980 to 1984, Shibu Soren kept on raising demand in Parliament for a separate Jharkhand state. In the meantime, Prime Minister Indira Gandhi was assassinated in October 1984. Rajiv Gandhi had taken over as prime minister. Public sympathy was in favour of Rajiv Gandhi and Congress.

Shibu Soren tried his luck again from Dumka only - this time under the banner of Jharkhand Mukti Morcha. However, luck did not favour him and he lost to the same Congress candidate Prithvi Chandra Kiskoo whom he had defeated in 1980. Shibu Soren's loss in this election did not have much significance, as even many legendary leaders had lost under the sympathy wave. Bihar was not yet divided then and Congress candidates had won all the seats in the present Jharkhand region.

Year 1985: Legislator from Jama

After losing the election in 1984, Shibu Soren was left with two options - wait for another five years to be a parliamentarian or become a legislator. The elections for Bihar Assembly were scheduled for next year i.e., 1985. He decided to contest from Jama assembly constituency. Though Shibu Soren had lost the parliamentary election in 1984, his movement had already put JMM on a strong footing in the entire Santhal Pargana region. This was even reflected in 1980 elections. In 1980, 11 legislators were elected from Jharkhand Mukti Morcha and most of them belonged to Santhal Pargana. Hence, Shibu Soren decided to contest

1985 assembly election. Whichever assembly seat (especially out of the seats that were already under control of JMM) he would have chosen to contest in Santhal Pargana, he would have definitely won; still he had chosen to contest from Jama. Jama was the constituency where Deven Soren had won in 1980 securing 19,636 votes. Even the winning margin was good. When Shibu Soren contested from the same Jama seat, he registered a grand victory securing 66.2% votes. Shibu Soren defeated Prem Murmu of Congress with a heavy margin. This election was quite beneficial for him, as his and his party's demand for a separate Jharkhand state kept echoing in the assembly after that.

Shibu Soren's decision to contest from Jama helped Jharkhand Mukti Morcha fare better in nearby regions also. Nine of their candidates secured victory; they included Simon Marandi from Littipara, Devidhan Besara from Maheshpur, David Murmu from Shikaripara, Stephen Marandi from Dumka, Shibu Soren himself from Jama, Suraj Mandal from Pauraiyahat, Sumarit Mandal from Godda, Salkhan Soren from Gandey and Krishna Mardi from Saraikela. Seven out of those 9 seats belonged to Santhal Pargana. This figure indicates how Santhal Pargana was a stronghold of Shibu Soren and Jharkhand Mukti Morcha.

Year 1989: Guruji Becomes Member of Parliament second time from Dumka

Time passed by and the 1989 Lok Sabha election approached. In the meantime, many significant incidents occurred in Jharkhand that helped Jharkhand Mukti Morcha in expanding its foothold. In 1987, Nirmal Mahto, President of Jharkhand Mukti Morcha, was murdered in Jamshedpur. Before that, AJSU was formed in 1986. The entire region was boiling after Nirmal Mahto's murder. The Jharkhand Movement was in full steam. Both JMM and AJSU launched major campaigns during these three years. In the meantime, the Jharkhand Coordination Committee was also constituted. The Jharkhand Movement had quickly spread to the entire region. The impact of the same was visible in 1989 parliamentary elections. By that time, Shibu Soren had taken over as the president of Jharkhand Mukti Morcha. Shibu Soren again contested from Dumka and defeated Congress candidate Prithvi Chandra Kiskoo by over 1,00,000 votes. Shibu Soren was a Member of Parliament for the second time. The number of votes for Shibu Soren increased from 1,02,535 in 1984 to 2,47,502 in 1989. For the first time, three candidates from Jharkhand Mukti Morcha had been elected as members of parliament. Besides Shibu Soren,

Shailendra Mahto, General Secretary of JMM, from Jamshedpur and Simon Marandi from Rajmahal had reached the parliament.

Year 1991: Defeated Babulal Marandi in Dumka

Within two years i.e., in 1991, parliamentary elections were held again. The Jharkhand Movement was in great momentum and its impact could be observed in the entire Jharkhand region. Hence, it was being anticipated that Jharkhand Mukti Morcha might increase its tally. In 1991 again, Shibu Soren decided to contest from Dumka. This time, the Bharatiya Janata Party fielded Babulal Marandi to rein in Shibu Soren. Before this, Shibu Soren had been fighting against Congress candidates only. This time, the fight was against Babulal Marandi. Babulal Marandi was a popular leader of BJP. He was close to the organisation. Hence, the fight was expected to be interesting. Shibu Soren had his own style of campaigning. He had a good hold in the villages. Shibu Soren very comfortably defeated Babulal Marandi in this election. The figures proved that Babulal Marandi had even failed to give a good fight. While Shibu Soren polled 2,60,169 votes, Babulal Marandi could secure only 1,26,528 votes. In fact, the entire Jharkhand was witnessing a swing in favour of JMM. JMM was able to grab

6 out of 14 parliamentary seats of Jharkhand in this election. All the three seats in Santhal Pargana were won by JMM. Besides Shibu Soren from Dumka, Suraj Mandal and Simon Marandi registered their victories from Godda and Rajmahal respectively. Other JMM leaders who became Members of Parliament were Binod Bihari Mahto from Giridih, Shailendra Mahto from Jamshedpur and Krishna Mardi from Singhbhum. For the first time, Jharkhand Mukti Morcha had demonstrated its strength in 1991 elections and made it loud and clear that this regional party could not be ignored any more.

Year 1996: Marandi lost again, Guruji became Parliamentarian for the fourth time

Five years passed in the blink of an eye and it was time for 1996 parliamentary elections. Dumka was proving to be an impregnable fort for Shibu Soren. He decided to contest from Dumka only. The opponent was Babulal Marandi - same party, same candidate. Both of them had already fought against each other in 1991. Babulal also had developed his popularity in Dumka. This time also, Shibu Soren won the contest. He retained his Dumka seat by defeating Babulal Marandi for the second successive time. Of course, the margin of victory had got reduced significantly. For a moment, it appeared that Shibu Soren might lose. He polled 1,65,411 votes against 1,59,933 secured by BJP candidate Babulal Marandi. That means, Shibu Soren had won by a margin of 5,478 votes only. This was an alarm bell for him. This significantly low margin had given a warning that the next election might witness the wind blowing in other direction.

Babulal Marandi was making constant efforts to checkmate Shibu Soren in Dumka. Shibu Soren had started contesting the parliamentary elections from Dumka in 1980 and leaving 1984 aside, had never lost the seat in any election.

Year 1998: Mid-term Poll: First victory for Babulal Marandi

Lok Sabha elections had to be conducted again in 1998 after fall of Atal Bihari Vajpayee government. Everybody was keeping an eye on Dumka seat, as while Dumka had been a stronghold of Shibu Soren, Babulal Marandi was also getting stronger constantly. The sympathy wave was also in favour of BJP on the account of the fall of Vajpayee government. In both of the last two elections in 1991 and 1996, Shibu Soren had registered victory over his main rival Babulal Marandi. However, tables were turned in 1998 parliamentary elections. This time, there was a wave in favour of Bharatiya Janata Party in Jharkhand region and it bagged 12 out of 14 seats. BJP had promised to constitute a separate Jharkhand state after coming to power in the centre. This had an impact on people. Babulal Marandi defeated Shibu Soren in Dumka. Babulal Marandi polled 2,77,344 votes against 2,64,778 votes secured by Shibu Soren. The margin of defeat was not much, especially keeping in mind the wave in favour of BJP. This was Shibu Soren's second defeat in Dumka.

Year 1999: Guruji's wife, instead of Guruji, as contestant

Another election had to be conducted within a year after fall of Vajpayee government. The elections were held in September-October 1999. BJP again fielded Babulal Marandi in Dumka. Marandi had won this seat in the previous election. There was some curiosity to see whether Babulal Marandi would be able to retain the seat. It was confirmed that Babulal Marandi was not going to face Guruji this time, as, after his defeat in 1998, Shibu Soren had got elected to Rajya Sabha in July 1998 with the support of Rashtriya Janata Dal; his election was however declared void later. He continued to be a Member of Rajya Sabha from 8 July 1998 to 18 July 2001. It was hardly a little over a year since he had gone to Rajya Sabha when this Lok Sabha election was announced. In this election, Jharkhand Mukti Morcha fielded Shibu Soren's wife Roopi Soren as its candidate. She faced Babulal Marandi. Babulal somehow managed to win the election with a margin of less than 5000 votes. This was his second successive victory from Dumka.

Went to Rajya Sabha with NDA support

Shibu Soren was with NDA government till some time before constitution of Jharkhand state. When the Jharkhand state bill was passed, he expected that he would be made the first chief minister of the state and NDA would support him; but that did not happen. Babulal Marandi of BJP became the first chief minister of the state and that resulted in development of differences between Jharkhand Mukti Morcha and BJP. Their estrangement disappeared in 2002 when Shibu Soren won Rajya Sabha election with the support of NDA only. Elections were being held for two seats in Jharkhand. Congress had fielded Sarfaraz Ahmed. BJP had extra votes. Babulal Marandi was the chief minister at that time. Shibu

Soren sought support from the NDA. The elections were to be held on 27 March 2002 and just one day before that i.e., on 26 March, Shibu Soren made an appearance at NDA meeting at Ranchi and sought their support. Nevertheless, Shibu Soren and Babulal Marandi had already talked about this earlier. NDA supported Shibu Soren and he won. He continued to be a member of Rajya Sabha from 10 April 2002 to 2 June 2002.

Guruji won from Dumka in the 2002 Mid-term Poll

Shibu Soren always wished to go to the parliament by winning Lok Sabha elections. However, if he does lose an election, he is not left with any option other than Rajya Sabha. Shibu Soren had become a Member of Rajya Sabha in April 2002. Had he so wished, he could have continued as Rajya Sabha member till 2008. However, it's quite difficult to understand Shibu Soren's politics. He got fed up with Rajya Sabha within 2-3 months only. When the by-election was announced for Dumka, he filed his papers to contest the same. In fact, Babulal Marandi had taken over as the chief minister of Jharkhand and he had resigned from his parliamentary seat from Dumka. The by-election was hence being held in Dumka. This was an interesting by-election. Shibu Soren's old associate Simon Marandi had joined Congress. Congress decided to field Shibu Soren's old associate Simon Marandi against him. Ramesh Hembram was also in the field as BJP candidate. It appeared that Shibu Soren might get overwhelmed, as JMM had lost to BJP in both the last two elections. Initially, everything appeared to be going against Shibu Soren. The news had spread that BJP and JMM had entered into an agreement. Congress only was doing this. People also had started to believe the same to a great extent, as he had been elected to Rajya Sabha just three months back with the support of BJP. The main contest appeared to be between Marandi and Congress only. An incident took place just around that time. BJP supporters attacked Shibu Soren. Though Shibu Soren escaped unhurt, this incident changed the entire scene of the election. Guruji started to make reference to that attack in every subsequent meeting. He started to gather people by beating the drum himself. A sympathy wave in his favour developed. The Adivasi community got united and stood in support of Guruji. When the results were announced, Guruji had won the election by over 90000 votes. Ramesh Hembram of BJP got second position and Simon Marandi was placed third. The entire team of BJP, including their ministers and parliamentarians had come to campaign against Shibu Soren in this election. Despite that, they could not defeat Shibu Soren.

2004 Elections: Shibu Soren won again

General elections were held again in 2004. Two years ago in the by-election held there Shibu Soren had, by registering his victory, made it clear that this was his old bastion and he had complete hold on the same. In 2004, BJP had fielded Sonelal Hembram to oppose Shibu Soren. In this election, the votes polled by Shibu Soren crossed the 3-lakh mark and reached the figure of 3,39,516 whereas Sonelal of BJP could secure only 2,24,480 votes. For Shibu Soren, it was a matter of satisfaction that the victory margin was over 1 lakh, i.e., 1,15,436.

Year 2009: Lost in Tamar while still holding chief minister's post

Nobody would have even thought that Shibu Soren would lose the election while still holding the office of the state chief minister. It was not that he had not lost any election earlier. He had already lost Lok Sabha elections to Prithvi Chandra Kiskoo and to Babulal Marandi in Dumka. He had also lost assembly election from

Tundi in 1977, but the loss of 2009 was hard to digest and difficult to believe. This time, Shibu Soren was holding the office of the chief minister and losing election while still holding that office appeared to be improbable. This could have been possible only with his own supporters indulging in backstabbing and playing some dirty tricks. The same thing had happened to Guruji when Tamar assembly election results were announced on 8 January 2009. Chief Minister Shibu Soren (also a UPA candidate) had lost the election by 8,973 votes. He was not defeated by NDA. He was in fact defeated by Jharkhand Party's candidate Raja Peter. Shibu Soren had polled just 25,154 votes even though he was a JMM candidate and had the support of other constituents of UPA including Congress. He had to bear the brunt of this defeat. He had assumed power on 27 August 2008 as the chief minister of Jharkhand for the second time. He was not a legislator then and he was required to become a member of the state assembly within a period of six months.

Shibu Soren had got hundreds of people - both within and outside his family, elected to the assembly and the parliament; however, when he needed a single seat in 2009, even his close associates indulged in theatricals. Nobody was ready to vacate his seat. Shibu Soren was looking for a safe seat. Some legislators did agree but their seats were such where he could have encountered problems. Even the suspended legislator from BJP Vishnu Bhaiya was ready to vacate his Jamtara seat for Shibu Soren. Time passed by in search of a safe seat and the election for Tamar assembly seat arrived. There was no way out. UPA proposed the name of Shibu Soren for Tamar seat. Shibu Soren had earlier made an announcement not to contest from Tamar. He had the knowledge of equations in Tamar. Tamar was a Munda dominated assembly constituency and Raja Peter had worked hard there for a long time. Hence, there was certainly some risk. Though it was believed during the election that the main contest would be between Shibu Soren and NDA candidate Vasundhara Munda, Raja Peter came out to be the dark horse. In a way, Shibu Soren got entangled in the game of Congress. Congress had pressurised Shibu Soren to agree to contest from Tamar. When it was a contest between UPA and NDA, what was the need for Enos Ekka belonging to the Jharkhand Party that was supporting UPA camp to jump into the field? By the time the results were declared, Shibu Soren also had understood the entire game, but it was too late. He had already lost the election. He did not have any option other than tendering his resignation. Finally, he resigned from the post of chief minister. This was a sad moment of his political life.

Year 2009: Defeated Sunil Soren to become parliamentarian

General elections were held in 2009. At that time, many court cases were in progress against Shibu Soren. He had to even go to jail. BJP fielded Sunil Soren to challenge him and launched campaign against him. They made all kinds of accusations including his jail terms and bribery; however, that did not have any impact on Guruji's supporters and voters. Guruji had entered the field with his *nagada*. He went on responding to each and every allegation. He understood the pulse of politics. Even in the election, he was able to make his supporters understand that whatever he had done was just to ensure a dignified and respectable life for the families of the Adivasis. Guruji said, "Whatever I did was just to get you a separate state. What have I not suffered? Besides enduring police beatings, I had to even go to jail." These words from Guruji had great impact on people and he won again. Though Sunil Soren gave a good fight, it was Shibu Soren who secured victory. The victory margin came down to 19,088 votes. Shibu Soren had polled 2,08,367 votes against 1,89,279 votes of Sunil Soren. Ramesh Hembram from

JVM also was in the field in this election and he had also polled reasonably good number of votes. Had Ramesh Hembram not contested, his 64,423 votes could have impacted the election result.

Year 2014: Shibu Soren won even under Modi wave

The entire country was going through the 'Narendra Modi wave' during the Lok Sabha elections of 2014. Even Jharkhand was having its impact. People were curious to know the fate of Shibu Soren's seat. In this election, BJP was able to grab 12 out of 14 seats of the state; however, Jharkhand Mukti Morcha retained the other two seats. Despite the Modi wave, Shibu Soren registered victory from Dumka with a margin of 39,030 votes. Shibu Soren had polled 3,35,815 votes whereas Sunil Soren, who was placed second, had secured 2,96,785 votes. Babulal Marandi of JVM was also in the field in this election. He had already won twice from the same Dumka seat, but he had to be content with third position this time. Votes polled by him also had come down. Babulal Marandi had secured 1,58,122 votes. Shibu Soren's victory in 2014 despite Modi wave proves that he has deep insight of the politics of Santhal Pargana; it's difficult to crack that. BJP has been however trying to defeat him in many elections.

Year 2019: Shibu Soren defeated by Sunil Soren

This election was also held under Modi wave. Shibu Soren was contesting from Dumka. He was being opposed by Sunil Soren. This was the third consecutive direct fight against Sunil. Sunil Soren was considered to be Shibu Soren's disciple. As Shibu Soren was able to register victory against Modi wave in 2014, people were expecting him to win in 2019 also. It's correct that Shibu Soren, on account of his old age, could not run a large-scale people-contact campaign that he earlier used to do in every election. He was just participating in programmes in a symbolic manner. On the other side, Sunil Soren of BJP was engaged in a planned campaign. Youth was in favour of Modi and this was reflected in the result also. Shibu Soren was defeated in his own stronghold by young leader Sunil Soren by a margin of 47,000 votes. It may be noted that just a few months before this election, Shibu Soren had celebrated his 75th birthday.

Went to Rajya Sabha again in 2020

Shibu Soren had to face defeat in 2019 Lok Sabha election in Dumka. It appeared to be his last election, but it was not like that. Jharkhand Mukti Morcha fielded him as its candidate when 2020 Rajya Sabha elections were announced. Shibu Soren was elected for Rajya Sabha. JMM had performed exceptionally well during 2019 assembly elections in Jharkhand and it was in power; hence, JMM did not even require support from other alliance partners for Shibu Soren. Shibu Soren polled adequate votes and he was elected to Rajya Sabha for the third time.

There was a peculiar thing about this election - this was held in Coronavirus pandemic period. Shibu Soren had filed his nomination papers around three months back, but Rajya Sabha elections had to be postponed due to Corona. Eventually, elections were held on 19 June 2020. All the legislators cast their votes with masks on their faces. Hemant Soren is in power in the state. JMM had majority of votes in its favour. Shibu Soren hence did not have any problem in registering his victory.

Shibu Soren in Pictures

Shibu Soren (just behind Chandrasekhar) with former Prime Minister Chandrasekhar

With the then Prime Minister Atal Bihari Vajpayee in 2000

With Sonia Gandhi during an election campaign

Shibu Soren with other legislators during a meeting in Patna

Shibu Soren being arrested during Jharkhand Movement

Respect for Guruji in the hearts of leaders of all parties. With former Chief Minister Raghubar Das

Shibu Soren himself waters his gardens and fields daily morning

Not lagging behind in photography also

Driving for pleasure

Shibu Soren on Harmonium. Spare moments during General Session of JMM at Jamshedpur in 2003.

Guruji's Family

Shibu Soren alias Guruji considers the people of entire Jharkhand as his family. He says, "Every individual living in Jharkhand is his family." He considers even the animals and other living beings in the forests as members of his family. He is a vegetarian. He has never killed any animal in his life. He lived in the forest among birds and animals only. He never took fish or meat. His father Sobaran Soren was a Gandhian. His mother Sona Manjhi was a homemaker. Shibu Soren was one among five brothers and two sisters. Rajaram Soren was the eldest among brothers. Next to him were Shibu Soren (Guruji himself), Shankar Soren, Lalu Soren and Ramu Soren. His two sisters were married in Chandil and Chandankyari respectively. Shibu Soren had married Roopi Soren of Chandil in 1963.

An old snap of Shibu Soren's family

Among his three sons - Durga Soren, Hemant Soren and Basant Soren, Durga Soren was the eldest. He died at an early age (only 40 years) on 21 May 2009. That was the saddest day in the life of Shibu Soren. That day, when Durga's mother went to wake him up, he had not responded even after repeated attempts. When all the members of the family assembled, it became apparent that Durga Soren was no more. Shibu Soren was in Delhi at that time. He was brought to Bokaro in a special flight. Durga was a legislator from Jama. Later, his wife Sita Soren was elected from the Jama assembly seat. Durga's death had shattered Shibu Soren. Shibu's second son Hemant Soren had by then entered politics. He continued Guruji's legacy. He became a legislator. Later, he served as deputy chief minister and then even as the chief minister of Jharkhand. He also served as a member of Rajya Sabha for some time. Guruji also has a daughter named Anjali Soren. She is also in politics and has already contested Lok Sabha election from Odisha.

Shibu Soren with Darga Soren and Hemant Soren

Hemant Soren has continued his father Shibu Soren's political legacy. As such, Shibu Soren is in any case supreme in Jharkhand Mukti Morcha, but Hemant Soren, as its working president, has taken over the responsibility of the party also. Basant Soren, younger brother of Hemant Soren, was also quite active in student politics and he later entered politics. Shibu Soren's wife Roopi Soren herself also was in politics, especially when Shibu Soren was engaged in legal battles. She even contested Lok Sabha election from Dumka but lost to Babulal Marandi. Soft-spoken Roopi Soren has enjoyed great respect even within the party. When Shibu Soren was running his movement in Tundi forests and the Police were looking for him, Roopi Soren had the responsibility of taking care of the entire family. Right from parenting of the kids to their schooling and education, Roopi Soren had taken care of everything herself. Supriyo Bhattacharya and Binod Pandey have been staying with them for a long time and serving not only the party but Guruji also. Shibu Soren treats them as members of his own family. They have always stood with him in all his moments of happiness or sorrow and hence, they enjoy Guruji's blessings.

Leaders Come Out From Shibu Training School

It is an undeniable fact that a substantive representation in Jharkhand politics is of the students from Shibu Training school. Jharkhand Mukti Morcha is an organization that has not only played a pivotal role in the movement for formation of a separate Jharkhand state but has also raised a lot of members in the legislative assembly and the Indian parliament. It also includes such MLAs and MPs who are no longer working along with Shibu Soren. They are now part of different parties and are MLAs, MPs and even ministers. They were either trained by Shibu Soren or were moulded and given an opportunity by the Jharkhand Mukti Morcha. It has always been an essential characteristic of Shibu Soren (Guruji) that once he accepts someone as one of his own, he considers and treats them as a part of his family for life. This is why he commands immense respect from the leaders and members of other parties as well. He is a tribal leader who is respected by everyone, even though sometimes they are compelled by party politics to give public statements criticizing him.

Some of these names include Arjun Munda, Stephen Marandi, Simon Marandi, Shailendra Mahto, Hemlal Murmu, Vidyut Mahto, Champai Soren etc. Arjun Munda was a part of the movement for the formation of separate Jharkhand state. He started his political career as a member of JMM and also became a member of the legislative assembly from JMM in 1995. Later he became a member of the BJP and went on to become the Chief Minister of Jharkhand. He also became a union minister and was a student of Shibu Soren's school. Similarly, Shailendra Mahto was the General Secretary (Central Committee) of Jharkhand Mukti Morcha. When Shibu Soren was the President of JMM, Shailendra Mahto was included among the powerful leaders of the party. He was considered very close to Shibu Soren. In 1989 and 1991, he became a member of parliament from Jamshedpur. Later he resigned from JMM and joined the BJP, but after joining the BJP he never became a member of parliament. His wife

Guruji with JMM leaders

is a two-time parliamentarian from Jamshedpur from BJP. Neither Arjun Munda nor Shailendra Mahto returned to Jharkhand Mukti Morcha after resigning from the party. Another name is that of Vidyut Mahto. He was a powerful JMM leader in Singhbhum. He became an MLA from Bahragora from Jharkhand Mukti Morcha but resigned from the party in 2014 to join BJP and went on to become an MP from Jamshedpur. In 2019, he became an MP from Jamshedpur again. All the above names are considered to be powerful leaders who shifted to BJP from JMM. All of them learned politics under Shibu Soren's wing. Sunil Mahto is no longer alive but he too was made an MP by Guruji from Jamshedpur.

There are many such leaders who were once close to Guruji but resigned from JMM for various reasons, became a part of other political parties but later came back to JMM. Stephen Marandi is also considered to be very close to Guruji and is a big leader of Santhal Pargana. He became an MLA many times but resigned from the party because once he was denied a party ticket. He fought as an independent candidate and defeated Hemant Soren. He went on to join Congress as well as JVM but later returned to JMM and Guruji accorded him the same respect and position. Proximity between Simon Marandi and Guruji goes back to those days when the latter used to live in and run his agitation from Tundi, and he used to visit Santhal Pargana from there. Simon Marandi was one the foremost leaders who played an important role in establishing Guruji in the Santhal Pargana. He is one of those few leaders who had established himself in the Santhal Pargana prior to Guruji. Once he got angry and left Guruji and also contested elections against him from Dumka for the Congress party. Later he joined BJP and contested the election only to be defeated. Some time later, the same Simon Marandi returned to

JMM. Guruji welcomed back the same person who had once contested elections against him, with full dignity. This shows how much Guruji values his old relationships. Another such name is Hemlal Murmu. He was one of the powerful leaders of JMM. He was elected MLA from JMM many times. Later he resigned from JMM and joined BJP but was not able to showcase the same potential in the party which he used to do in JMM.

Yes, there are also such MLAs who did not leave Guruji even in the worst of times. Champai Soren and Ramdas Soren are such leaders. The number of such leaders is also huge. When somebody leaves Guruji, he is pained but when the same person returns, he showers the same love upon him or her. Such is Shibu Soren's (Guruji's) nature.

Guruji Wanted to Hoist Black Flags

During the agitation, there were many times when the protestors had announced that unless their demand of a separate Jharkhand state was fulfilled, they would boycott all programmes on 15th August and 26th January. They threatened to hoist black flags on these days and even attempts were made for the same. One such incident occurred on 15th August 1988. On that day, Shibu Soren was arrested following an attempt to hoist a black flag in Ranchi. Shibu Soren had already announced that if a separate Jharkhand state was not formed then all the programmes for 15th August will be boycotted and black flags will be hoisted. Workers of Jharkhand Mukti Morcha assembled at the party office in Bariatu road in Ranchi under Soren's leadership and a procession started from there. This procession reached Albert Ekka Chowk. Heavy police forces were deployed at Albert Ekka Chowk but the party workers outnumbered them. They broke the police barricading and garlanded the statue of Albert Ekka. When the procession started to move towards Bari ground police stopped them at Durgabari. Shibu Soren was arrested along with 115 party workers and they were taken to police station in government buses. Later a second batch of JMM workers started to move forward but the police stopped them and did not let anyone hoist black flags at Bari ground. After keeping them at police station for the entire day, all of them were released in the evening. In those days, such incidents during the movement for a separate Jharkhand state was very common and therefore police used to arrest people in processions and rallies and release them in the evening.

Order to leave Dhanbad

During the Jharkhand agitation, many such incidents had occurred that compelled the police to arrest Guruji, or a bounty was announced for his capture. In 1992, one such incident occurred in Dhanbad after which Guruji was ordered to leave the city. The unfateful incident occurred on 29th October 1992. Lalu Prasad Yadav was the then Chief Minister of Bihar. He was a vociferous opponent of a separate Jharkhand state. It was only a few days ago that he had made a statement that he would not allow Bihar to be divided and Jharkhand will be formed only over his dead body. Members of the Jharkhand Mukti Morcha were angered following this statement. During those days, tensions were so high that even small incidents would take a violent turn. On that day Guruji (Shibu Soren) was going to address a meeting at Barbadda Chowk in Dhanbad. Construction work was going on at the national highway. On the same day Chief Minister Lalu Prasad Yadav's caravan moved towards the airport after inspecting the construction work in Topachanchi. Jharkhand Mukti Morcha workers came to know about this. They assembled there and started pelting stones at the Chief Minister's caravan. A few arrows were also shot. The caravan was led by the vehicle of Superintendent of Police and CM's bodyguards were also seated in the same vehicle. They were injured in this entire ruckus. Following this, the police lathi charged the workers. Angry workers started pelting stones again. Police also fired a few shots in air. In the mean time, workers of Janta Dal also reached there and the workers of both the parties started a brawl among themselves. Somehow police managed to take Lalu Prasad Yadav out of there through a different route. Since the incident put a question on the security of chief minister, the administration retaliated strictly and Shibu Soren was taken in custody and later ordered to leave Dhanbad immediately in order to avoid further tension.

Bill Passed, Dream Comes True

Shibu Soren took up the reins of Jharkhand Mukti Morcha after the assassination of Nirmal Mahto in 1987. Till 1995, the Jharkhand Movement saw many ups and downs. Many incidents like bandhs, economic blockades, even blowing up of electric towers and railway tracks occurred during this time. It also saw statements from the home minister that a separate state is the only solution on one hand whereas on the other hand the chief minister said that a separate Jharkhand could be formed only over his dead body. Talks were held; sometimes in Patna and sometimes in Delhi. Amidst all these the movement also kept gathering momentum. It also witnessed incidents of passing of separate state bills from the Bihar legislative assembly, forwarding it to the central government for consent and the same being returned to the Bihar government. Political parties also kept changing their stands during this time. Those political parties that were against a separate Jharkhand state became a supporter and joined the movement under public pressure. It included the BJP and the Congress as well. Relations between AJSU and JMM also saw good and bad times. The Jharkhand Coordination Committee was formed under B P Kesari but initially it failed to take JMM along with it. The formation of the Jharkhand Area Autonomous Council did bring a little relief but it was also another milestone. Real happiness came when the Jharkhand bill was passed in the Lok Sabha in 2000 and the dream of a separate Jharkhand was realized.

Actually, the year 2000 was a special year for the Jharkhand movement as well as Shibu Soren. A long-time dream of a separate Jharkhand state was realized that year. In those days, Shibu Soren (Jharkhand Mukti Morcha) was a part of National Democratic Alliance (NDA) and the JMM supported Nitish Kumar in forming the government in the state. At that time, he was assured that after the formation of Jharkhand he will become the chief minister of the state, but it did not happen. When a political battle was ongoing in Bihar and betrayal day (vishwasghat diwas) was being observed at that time NDA sat on a protest at J P circle in Patna on 13th March 2000. In that protest, Shibu Soren also sat along with Nitish Kumar. Political circumstances were very different in those times. The Rabri Devi government was opposing a separate Jharkhand state. Nitish Kumar and NDA were in favour of Jharkhand. In that protest Shibu Soren said, "In order to oppose the partition of Bihar, Lalu Prasad is terrorizing the people of Bihar for no reason. Both Haryana and Punjab are prosperous after the partition of Punjab." He had also said that he will remain a part of NDA because NDA is committed to the formation of Jharkhand. In that protest, Shibu Soren also attacked Congress and said that a fierce and powerful movement will be launched against Congress in Jharkhand. Saryu Rai was also present in this meeting. The main reason behind such a ferocious attack against Congress and RJD was that in those days JMM was a part of the NDA.

Shibu Soren Conducts a Rally in Delhi

The month of July was coming to an end. The Winter session of Parliament was going on. Shibu Soren wanted that the government should introduce the Jharkhand bill in the parliament as soon as possible and the matter was getting prolonged from the government's side. In order to pressurize the government Shibu Soren decided to conduct a rally in Delhi. More than a thousand people from Jharkhand arrived in Delhi for this purpose. Simon Marandi, Stephen Marandi, Hemant Soren, Hemlal Murmu, Sudhir Mahto, Teklal Mahto, Champai Soren, Abu Talim Ansari, Rajendra Mehta, Sunil Mahto, Arjun Ram among others had arrived from Jharkhand in order to participate in this rally. On 25th July 2000, the rally started from Shibu Soren's official residence in Delhi. When this procession started to move towards the parliament from Jantar Mantar, it was stopped by the police. Addressing this rally, Shibu Soren gave out a warning and said that if the state of Jharkhand was not formed in the monsoon session of the parliament, he would not let coal, iron ore and other minerals from Jharkhand go out to other states. Although he also hoped that a bill for Jharkhand would be introduced in the Lok Sabha on that very day, i.e. 25th July 2000. This is exactly what happened. After the rally in the day, the Jharkhand state bill was introduced in the Lok Sabha in the evening. Amidst opposition from a few parties, home minister Lal Krishna Advani introduced the bill for the formation of separate states of Jharkhand, Uttaranchal and Chhattisgarh. That was a historic moment for

Jharkhand. Now, it was the time for debate on the bill and getting it passed.

Shibu Soren's Hard Stance

Even before its introduction, the bill was facing an opposition from Jharkhand. Members from the state were demanding that Saraikela - Kharsawan should be acceded to Orissa instead of making it a part of Jharkhand. At that time Biju Janta Dal (BJD) was a part of NDA and so was the JMM. After this stubborn approach from BJD, Shibu Soren also took a tough stand and made it very clear that if BJD does not drop its demand to make Saraikela Kharsawan a part of Orissa, JMM will also raise a demand to make Mayurbhanj, Kyonjhar and Sundargarh a part of Jharkhand. Actually, these three districts are a part of greater Jharkhand. BJD has gone to the extent of saying that if Saraikela-Kharsawan was not made a part of Orissa, it would withdraw its support from the NDA. Shibu Soren made it very clear that under no circumstances BJD's demand will be made and that they should immediately stop threatening the alliance. After this, BJD gave up its demand.

Prior to BJD, RJD was also singing its own tune. Yes, Congress was in support. At that time Congress was in alliance with the RJD government. There were ministers from Jharkhand as well. Angry with RJD's attitude one day Pradeep Balmuchu and Dev Kumar Dhan made it very clear that if the RJD does not agree then they will resign from the government. After this, Balmuchu went to Delhi to meet Sonia Gandhi and requested her to support the Jharkhand bill in the parliament. Sonia Gandhi assured him. After the assurance from Congress the road to pass the bill seemed clear. At this time opposition from small parties like RJD and BJD became irrelevant.

Shibu Soren was sitting in the Viewer's Gallery

The fateful day of 2nd August 2000 had arrived. Jharkhand bill was being debated. On this historic occasion Shibu Soren was sitting in the viewer's gallery of the Lok Sabha. At that time, he was not a member of the Lok Sabha. Along with his companions his jubilation was evident from the gallery. Almost all the stalwart leaders of Bihar and Jharkhand were present in the gallery on that day. Apart from Shibu Soren, Bihar BJP President Nand Kishore Yadav, Sushil Modi, Subodhkant Sahay, Sarayu Rai, Shailendra Mahto, Dr Ramdayal Munda, Arjun Munda, Durga Soren, Pradeep Balmuchu, Sarfaraz Ahmad, Deepak

Prakash, C P Singh were also present. After a long debate, the Jharkhand bill was finally passed from the Lok Sabha on the night of 2nd August. Entire Jharkhand was jubilated.

Shibu Soren's First Message

On one hand many people were fighting for, giving sacrifices, were being beaten up and shot at by the police for Jharkhand but there were also such people who were against the new state. Although their number was very low but as the road to the formation of Jharkhand was getting clearer a question was also rising – what will happen after the formation of Jharkhand? Will the people who have come from outside be thrown out of the state? Or how will they be treated? These apprehensions were not unfounded as armed demonstrations during the movement were very common. Bandhs, economic blockades, arson, sabotage and tearing up the railway tracks were very common. Therefore, on one hand there were people who were rejoicing on the formation of Jharkhand on the other hand there were people who were apprehensive about the future of non-Jharkhand residents. But it was very important to restore a positive environment in Jharkhand after the formation of the state. Shibu Soren was also aware of this and therefore he put forth his views very clearly. After listening to him all the apprehensions were cleared away. Immediately after the bill was passed, I congratulated him and requested him to address the people residing in Jharkhand. I spoke to him over telephone on the night of 2nd August. He had said that it is a result of the sacrifices of the ancestors that today we are getting the state of Jharkhand. No one should fear the formation of Jharkhand. He also said that the entrepreneurs from other states are also welcome to establish their enterprises in Jharkhand. They will be given complete security and all the amenities like electricity, water etc. Businessmen from other states will also be welcomed. Family members of those who were martyred for the formation of Jharkhand will be taken care of. These statements by Shibu Soren were published in the newspapers the following morning. It sent out a positive message.

On 3rd August, Shibu Soren gave more clarity to his statements. Initially Shibu's entire movement was directed against powerbrokers, moneylenders and mafia. Therefore, immediately after the formation of the state he did not hesitate in warning such elements. I spoke to him over telephone on 3rd August as well. He had said 'no peaceful resident will be driven out of Jharkhand.' Issuing a stern warning to the exploiters, criminals and mafia he had said, 'they should mend their ways or else they shall be driven out of Jharkhand. Jharkhand will be a place for peaceful people only and there will be no place for criminals here.' Guruji had said those who are settled here, are born here, have adopted Jharkhand's culture, they are all Jharkhandi. Those who have come from outside the state and are peace loving, they also have no reason to fear. No one should have misconception that they will receive a step-motherly treatment. He had also said 'everybody residing in Jharkhand is a Jharkhandi. It is because of the combined efforts of all the people of the state that today we are getting a separate state. Therefore, after we get this separate state, we will make it a paradise and establish Ram Rajya here. Those who have come from North Bihar or any other part outside the state, are running their business should not be worried at all. They will not face any difficulty. They should honestly work for the prosperity and growth of the region.' He said that it is not that Jharkhand belongs to tribal people only. Both the tribal and non-tribal have fought together for the formation of the state and have got it. Therefore, the question of confrontation between the two does not arise. When all are Jharkhandi then where is the place for confrontation. Those who left Jharkhand for political reasons should now return to Jharkhand. Everybody will be safe here. Two days after the Jharkhand bill was passed in the parliament, Shibu Soren had sent a message to the entire state that Jharkhand will be free of all fears.

Could Not Become the First Chief Minister

Since the day Jharkhand bill was passed in the Lok Sabha, i.e., 2nd August 2000, contention claims and counter claims for the post of Chief Minister of Jharkhand started to pour in. Shibu Soren, who had fought a long and hard battle for Jharkhand was already the strongest contestant of all of them. At that time, he was a part of the NDA. BJP was keeping its cards very close to its chest. With 32 members, BJP had the highest number of MLAs in the Jharkhand assembly. They also had the support of 8 MLAs of JDU and Samata party. Their total number was reaching 40 and they were only one short of majority. Reaching the majority mark was not a tough ask for the NDA but Shibu Soren had already put forth his claim. He had said that he was promised the post of chief minister by the NDA once Jharkhand came into existence, therefore he should be given a chance. Actually Shibu Soren was reminding the NDA of the post election circumstances and JMM's support to the NDA. Elections were held for Bihar legislative assembly in March 2000 and no party or alliance was able to attain majority and a hung assembly was formed. Despite being 40 short of the majority mark erstwhile Governor Binod Chandra Pandey swore in Nitish Kumar as the Chief Minister. At that time JMM had 12 MLAs. Shibu Soren was also asked to extend his support. In return, Shibu Soren put forth the condition that after the formation of government a bill regarding the formation of separate Jharkhand state should be passed from Bihar legislative assembly and be sent to the central government. Chief Minister Nitish Kumar expressed his commitment for the formation of Jharkhand through the Governor's address to the assembly. JMM also supported this. Despite this Nitish Kumar could not attain majority and during the debate he resigned. Later, Rabri Devi swore in as the Chief Minister of the state. When the Jharkhand bill was passed from the Lok Sabha, Shibu Soren put forth his claim for the post of chief minister saying that he was assured that after the formation of Jharkhand, he only would be made the chief minister by NDA. He had extended his support to Nitish Kumar on this condition.

At that time, the RJD government was functional with the support of Congress and other parties in Bihar. RJD leader Lalu Prasad Yadav was very well aware that the bill was passed and there was nothing he could do, but he wanted to stop BJP from coming to power. Therefore, without any further delay he called Shibu Soren on 3rd August 2000 and spoke to him over telephone. He offered him the post of Chief Minister provided he steps out of NDA. He assured him of UPA's support. Although when Lalu Yadav made this offer to Shibu Soren, the latter was a part of NDA. UPA was acting as per their own plans. Its first step was to somehow prepare JMM to leave NDA. A day earlier Mohsina Kidwai, a tall leader of the Congress party had made a public statement that their first priority would be to stop BJP from coming to power. At that time, Chandan Bagchi was the acting President of the Bihar Pradesh Congress Committee. He had also said that they will try to stop the BJP. On one hand Congress was already acting according to its plans on the other hand Lalu was also not sitting idle either. He talked to Congress leader Ajit Jogi over telephone from Bihar Bhawan situated in Delhi and assured him that a plan was being worked out. On 4th August also he talked to Shibu Soren over telephone and assured him of his support.

Shibu Soren has been a clever politician as well. He was very well aware that BJP is not going to make him the Chief Minister easily. Therefore, he remained in contact with the leaders of UPA so that NDA could feel the pressure. Initially all the leaders from NDA were keeping their mouths shut on this issue. Shibu Soren also did not want to take any decision in haste. Although he was giving statements, mounting pressure but he was not showing any hurry to quit NDA. One change was quite visible. After getting signals from UPA his tone was slowly getting harder. Shibu Soren returned to Ranchi on 8th August 2000. He received an overwhelming welcome. Just like a hero. Even in Ranchi one question was repeatedly asked of him – will he become the Chief Minister? Initially he kept his silence but as his patience grew thinner, he said – "Did I start the movement to graze cattle"? This statement from Shibu Soren was enough to show that he was not willing to let go his claim. He was confident that the JDU leaders will support him. A few other small parties who were a part of the Jharkhand Movement will also come along. On the other side, BJP was also very quietly working according to its plans and its leaders were giving very calculated statements.

AJSU also had two members – Sudesh Mahto and Joba Manjhi. AJSU also did not want Shibu Soren to become the Chief Minister. BJP leaders were also aware of this. BJP and AJSU reached a consensus on the next move and its timing. AJSU had openly declared that both its MLAs will not be a part of the alliance that supports Shibu Soren. This happened on 10th August. Thus by that time it was evidently clear that JMM can issue its statements but AJSU will not comply with it.

Shibu Soren came to Delhi to decide the future politics. Although on 11th August Shibu Soren had clearly said that it was NDA which had formed the state of Jharkhand hence it was their prerogative to decide the chief minister but he also added that Chief Minister should be someone who had taken part in the agitation, who has sacrificed, who knows Jharkhand and someone who has gone to jail for the movement. In his own way Shibu Soren hads said all that he wanted to say. Next day a function was organized at Shibu Soren's official residence in Delhi. In this function, the responsibility to solve the dispute of chief minister was put upon Nitish Kumar and George Fernandes as these two leaders were said to have given the assurance to Shibu Soren earlier. There was a hustle and bustle going on in BJP as well. On 13th August 2000, when Kariya Munda arrived at Ranchi airport, he was given a grand welcome which was similar to that of a chief minister. He was brought to Albert Ekka Chowk from Sankatmochan Mandir on a wooden elephant. On 17th August former BJP president Kushabhau Thackeray on his way to Delhi, stayed in Ranchi for a day. This matter was brought in front of him as well. Then he had said only one thing that NDA will form the government.

Now everything was lying on the statements made by the leaders of NDA in response to assurance claims made by Shibu Soren. Kushabhau Thackeray had also not said anything clearly and on 18th August Govindacharya had said that he had no knowledge about whether Shibu Soren was given any kind of assurance or not. It was not only the statement from Govindacharya but BJP leader Sushil Modi took one step further and said that JMM is a supporting party and not an ally. The way statements were being made things were getting clearer that BJP was slowly showing its cards and creating an environment. On 19th August 2000 a meeting of state BJP MLAs was called in which Kushabhau Thackeray was also present. In his talks with the MLAs, he said that central leadership will decide the chief minister. On one hand BJP was measuring its every word and taking its time whereas on the other hand UPA had publicly announced JMM or Shibu Soren's name for chief minister. Amidst all this, Shailendra Mahto (who had been an MP from BJP earlier and his wife was a BJP MP at the time of formation of state) demanded that only Shibu Soren, who had fought a long battle for the state should be made the chief minister. Camp building had started. The erstwhile union finance minister, Yashwant Sinha arrived in Ranchi on 20th August. Very clearly, he stated that neither NDA nor the central leadership had ever promised Shibu Soren that he will be made the chief minister. If Nitish Kumar or George Fernandes had made any such promise then he was not aware of it. After this statement from Yashwant Sinha it became very clear that BJP would not give the CM's post to Shibu Soren. Replying to this statement from Yashwant Sinha, Shibu Soren made only one statement that JMM was still a part of NDA. Although Shibu Soren was not speaking openly against the NDA, Durga Soren gave out a clear statement that if NDA would not make Guruji the chief minister then they will talk to others. Durga was indicating towards UPA but Guruji was taking every step very cautiously. In between all this Guruji called upon Lal Krishna Advani in his office in parliament on 21st August. Guruji did not seem satisfied with the meeting. It was evident that even Advani could not do anything to help him in this matter. Now Shibu

Soren had no other option but to meet Prime Minister Atal Bihari Vajpayee and speak his mind in front of him. A meeting of BJP's working committee was scheduled to be held in Nagpur. Meeting with Vajpayee was possible only after the meeting. Guruji even waited for that. In between, Guruji presided over a meeting of MLAs in Delhi in which JMM had taken a relatively tough stand. Very clearly, it asked BJP if they are willing to make Guruji chief minister or not? Now this issue could not be prolonged any further.

Sonia Gandhi moves forward

UPA and NDA both were maneouvering for the post of chief minister but the bill had still not gotten the President's assent. Congress showed its seriousness on 24th August when Sonia Gandhi gave Ajit Jogi the responsibility to form government in Jharkhand. Although, Ajit Jogi and Shibu Soren had already held talks earlier. On 29th August Sonia Gandhi had even called a meeting of MLAs of Jharkhand in Delhi. Congress' biggest worry was the fact that JMM was still a part of NDA. Shibu Soren was also meeting with BJP leaders on one hand while on the other hand he was also meeting leaders of other allies of NDA. On 25th August Shibu Soren met Lal Krishna Advani and

Sharad Yadav and later returned to Dhanbad on 29th August. He held a public meeting there and returned to Ranchi. By that time state president of Samta Party, Raghunath Jha had also arrived in Ranchi. He had already made a statement that Shibu Soren is charge sheeted therefore he could not be supported. To this Guruji replied that when one is involved in a movement then there will be charge sheets and cases against him, but until he is penalized it is not right to call him a criminal.

BJP framed me

Time was running out. Shibu Soren remained in NDA and had made all the efforts possible. On 13th October he was in Kahalgaon. Simon Marandi was also accompanying him. Now it was only month to the formation of Jharkhand and the appointment of a new chief minister, but Shibu Soren had sensed that BJP will not let him become the chief minister and will keep on passing the time. Then he started to attack BJP. That day i.e., on 13th October Guruji clearly alleged that in order to keep his party away from power, BJP is trying to frame him (Shibu Soren) in parliamentarian bribery case. JMM had a clear claim on the post of chief minister and that he would not let it go at any cost. That day Guruji was in an attacking mood. There were things that were buried deep in his heart but he could not share till now; he started to speak about them in Kahalgaon. Although till that day JMM was a part of NDA but a disgruntled Guruji tried to indicate that RJD – Congress way was also open for him when along with Atal Bihari Vajpayee he also credited Lalu Yadav and Sonia Gandhi for the formation of Jharkhand. He wanted that RJD – Congress should be the last resort and that all the options should be tried first while remaining in NDA. Hence, he made a public statement that NDA and BJP are not one and the same. There are other parties in the alliance as well and they should also speak out their mind.

The foundation stone for Guruji's claim for the position of chief minister was the assurance given to him. Guruji had always maintained that he was given assurance by the leaders of JDU. Everything was now dependent upon the JDU but Guruji took a huge blow when Nitish Kumar, on 15th October in Dhanbad, said that no assurance was given to Shibu Soren in return of his support to NDA. At that time Nitish Kumar was the agriculture minister in the Vajpayee government. It was the first time that such statement came from Nitish Kumar. After this statement from Nitish Kumar it was very clear that NDA will never let Shibu

Soren become the chief minister and they did not care if JMM remained a part of NDA or not.

Shibu Soren had never been a leader who would give up easily. He knew the path of struggle very well and on 22nd October 2000 he addressed a huge public gathering in Ranchi to display his might. Guruji gave a call to his party workers and asked them to be ready for a decisive battle on 15th November. He also gave a call to the youth of Jharkhand asking them to be present in Ranchi at any cost; he added that if their choice of CM was not appointed then they should prepare for another battle.

Meeting with Vajpayee and Fernandes

On 22nd October 2000, Guruji addressed a historic rally at Morabadi ground in Ranchi and made a fiery speech in his old flavour. A huge crowd had gathered to listen to him that day. The scenes at the Morabadi ground bore uncanny similarity to the days of the Jharkhand agitation. The aggression displayed by Guruji in his speech could be understood from the excerpts of his speech. 'Jharkhand will be run by Jharkhandis and not outsiders. New Jharkhand shall belong to common man, it should belong to you and me and not some factory owner. If the station in-charge does not listen encompass (gherao) the police station, pull him from his chair and seat yourself. No alarms shall ring in police stations but only the dugdugi will beat. If any DC or SP or DFO does not listen to you 50000 people should encompass him and decide his fate then and there'. These excerpts from his speech show his might and the its ability to mobilise the forces as he used to give the same speeches in 1973-74 when he ran a parallel government in Tundi and nearby areas. After this speech, it did not seem that Guruji was willing to talk to the leaders of NDA anymore but he also did not want to quit trying to find a way through talks. This is why he decided to meet first George Fernandes and then Atal Bihari Vajpayee and put his point of view in front of them. At that time George Fernandes was the convener of NDA.

Shibu Soren was to meet George Fernandes along with his supporters on 27th October but this meeting could not happen. The meeting was deffered by George Fernandes because he received a message that BJP could make some important announcement regarding the Chief Minister on 6th November. George wanted that before he met Shibu Soren, everything should be clear so that he could say things clearly to Guruji. For this, George wanted to meet and discuss the issue with top leaders of BJP first. Erstwhile BJP president

Bangaru Laxman called Kailashpati Mishra to Delhi. BJP's top leadership also wanted to discuss the issue with top state leaders of BJP. There were two contenders for the position of chief minister from BJP – Kariya Munda and Babulal Marandi. There was partisanship even within the party over these two names. Guruji also understood the situation. Deferring the meeting with George and calling the BJP leaders to Delhi were indicating that things were moving away. Guruji also did not want to waste his time sitting in Delhi. Therefore, he called meeting of JMM MLAs on 1st November in Patna. On the other side BJP leaders were assembling Delhi. As the date of 1st November was approaching the matter of discussion in BJP was not whether the chief minister will be from BJP or JMM but whether the chief minister will be Kariya Munda or Babulal Marandi.

Vajpayee–Soren meeting

After the meeting of JMM MLAs in Patna, the party gave an ultimatum to BJP that it should clarify if it wants to make Shibu Soren the Chief Minister or not. JMM went to the extent of saying that if BJP is not ready then it should say clearly so that JMM has no issues in taking a decision (about quitting NDA). After attending the meeting in Patna, Guruji went to Delhi to meet George Fernandes on 3rd November and once again put forward his claim for the position of Chief Minister stating that at the time of formation of Nitish Government, he was assured that whenever Jharkhand will be formed, he only will become the chief minister of the state. George listened to Guruji very calmly but made no promises. Shibu Soren also did not want to leave any stone unturned therefore he wanted to meet Atal Bihari Vajpayee as the last resort. Guruji wanted JMM to take the final call only after his meeting with Atal Bihari Vajpayee. Finally, that day also arrived. The day of 4th November 2000. Guruji met Vajpayee, took his blessings and put his point in front of him. The meeting between them continued for half an hour. Vajpayee listened to Guruji very calmly but did not make any assurances from his side. This meeting was very important because Kariya Munda had also met Vajpayee a day earlier. They had an old and special relationship. Therefore, this meeting was also seen in a different way. After Guruji's meeting with Vajpayee, a rumour started doing rounds that JMM has agreed to let go the post of chief minister in return for position of deputy chief minister. However, on the same day, Guruji himself said "Can an inspector become a watchman"?

Thus, it was understood that Guruji will not back down from his decision.

Announcement to quit NDA

5th November was a decisive day. A day earlier, the meeting between Guruji and Vajpayee had taken place. Till that time JMM had decided that whatever the decision might be, the decision to quit will be thought upon in the meeting of working committee of JMM which was scheduled to be held in Patna on 7th November. It meant that two days still remained. In between this, on the same day, a meeting between George Fernandes and Vajpayee took place. George talked to Guruji for almost two hours. Yashwant Sinha and Digvijay Singh were also present in this meeting. This meeting also ended with no result. While BJP was busy with its preparations, by the evening JMM got the message that BJP will not make Shibu Soren chief minister, even if JMM quits NDA. As soon as they received the indications, without waiting any further R. K. Anand, on behalf of JMM announced the withdrawal of support from NDA. It was Anand who clarified that since NDA is not ready to make Shibu Soren the chief minister therefore it was no longer sensible to remain in NDA. He also announced quitting NDA. It was thought that JMM will announce the withdrawal after the meeting of the working committee, but it did not happen. When Anand made this announcement, Guruji was not present there.

It was now clear that JMM has chosen a different path and it had no other option but to seek support from UPA. JMM started making those efforts. BJP faced only one problem – who should they make the Chief Minister-- Marandi or Munda? Even the top leadership was divided. Vajpayee and Kailashpati Mishra were in favour of Kariya Munda whereas Advani, Joshi and most of the MLAs were supporting Marandi. Kariya Munda's supporters were saying that it's not only about the position of Chief Minister but of the Lok Sabha seat as well. If Marandi becomes the chief minister, he will have to vacate Dumka seat and it will not be easy for BJP to win that seat back but Khunti seat that will be vacated by Munda will be easy to win. However, this argument was not taken very seriously.

Guruji's Proposition to Kariya Munda

On 9th November, a meeting of BJP MLAs took place in Patna and all the speculations were put to rest when Babulal Marandi was elected as the leader of BJP. On the same day Kariya Munda also met Vajpayee. He was offered a position in central cabinet which he refused. By 12th

November, Guruji had understood that despite getting support from UPA, he will not be able to become the first chief minister of Jharkhand. Numbers were not in his favour. Guruji was also aware that Kariya Munda was angry. He also had the support of a few MLAs with him. Therefore, on 12th November Guruji sent message to Kariya Munda and said to him that if the latter becomes chief minister then JMM will support him. In the same night I talked to Kariya Munda over telephone from Jamshedpur on this matter. I explained to him that Shibu Soren has given such a statement. Would he like to say something on this proposition? At that time, he was in Delhi. He did not take this proposition very seriously and said, "Now it's too late. If Shibu Soren had to say something, he should have said it a little earlier. Now there is no point in saying anything." When I repeatedly asked him he replied, "In a couple of days I am coming to Ranchi and will talk there."

Kariya Munda is an experienced politician and if BJP had decided on the name of Marandi then there was nothing he could do. Also, he would not even think of going against the party decision therefore he gave this statement to brush the matter aside. On the day of swearing -in ceremony, apart from stalwarts from Congress, Lalu Yadav had also arrived in Ranchi. A meeting was held in Ashoka hotel but they could not get the required numbers. Even moments before the swearing-in a political stir happened in the Raj Bhavan but finally Governor Prabhat Kumar put everything to rest and swore Babulal Marandi in as the first Chief Minister of Jharkhand. With this, curtains were brought down on a three and half month-long political drama.

Long Power is Never Found

It is the truth that the time devoted by Shibu Soren for the movement of a separate Jharkhand state is more than any other leader but he was not destined to enjoy power for long. Several times he

Shibu Soren taking oath as Chairman of JAAC. Next to him is Suraj Mandal.

got hold of the seat of power but it slinked away from his hands even quicker. Other than the post of the chairman just before the formation of Jharkhand, whenever he became the chief minister of Jharkhand (three times) or central minister, he could never complete his full term. It was his ill fate that every time he had to vacate his office due to one reason or another.

Became the chairman of JAAC on 9th August 1995

Shibu Soren was fighting a battle for a separate state of Jharkhand. In between, many other options were also put forward. Some were talking about a development council, someone was advising the status of union territory while some were also talking about autonomous council. Those who were not in favour of a separate Jharkhand state were giving different advices in order to delay the matter. But for how long could the matter be delayed? Demand for a separate Jharkhand was entrenched deep in the minds of its people. Similarly, the agitators also believed strongly that one day Jharkhand will have to be given to them. If it is getting delayed due to any reason, they should grab whatever they are getting. In this process, the Jharkhand Area Autonomous Council was formed. On 9th August 1995, Shibu Soren took oath as its chairman. This function was organized in the Morabadi ground in Ranchi. Suraj Mandal became the deputy chairman. Later, the post of the chairman of JAAC was considered equivalent to the post of Chief Minsiter. Although there was a dilemma regarding JAAC from the beginning, many companions of Shibu Soren had refused to become a part of JAAC. It included Shailendra Mahto and Krishna Mardi as well. JAAC was the first bivouac. After five years, a separate state of Jharkhand was formed.

On 2nd March 2005 he became the Chief Minister for the First Time

When a separate state of Jharkhand was formed on 15th November 2000, everybody thought that Shibu Soren would become the first Chief Minister of the state as he had devoted 40 years of his life for the movement, but it did not happen. Situation and numbers were not in his favour. BJP trumped him and Babulal Marandi became the first chief minister of the state. Shibu Soren had to wait for almost four years to become the chief minister of Jharkhand. He became the chief minister on 2nd March 2005. His disciple Arjun Munda became the chief minister before him, even though he was from BJP. Although Shibu Soren became the chief minister but the political circumstances were such that he could remain in office for 10 days only.

Shibu Soren taking oath as Chief Minister for the first time.

UPA did not get a clear mandate in the elections held in 2005. Independents held the key. On 1st March 2005, a letter containing list of 41 MLAs supporting Arjun Munda was given to Governor Syed Sibtey Razi but the Governor asked Arjun Munda to wait. Next day, all of a sudden, he swore Shibu Soren in along with six other ministers. Not only this, but he also gave Guruji time till 21st March to prove his majority in the house. When this decision of the Governor faced serious opposition, he replied that this decision was based on his discretion and not numbers. Stephen Marandi, Girinath Singh, Joba Manjhi,

Bandhu Tirki, Annapurna Devi and Kamlesh Singh also took oath along with Guruji. NDA leaders and then governor Sibtey Razi went on to the extent of saying that if NDA has the majority they should topple the government on 21st March. NDA took an aggressive stance on this issue and declared the governor directly guilty. The atmosphere in the entire state was against the governor. He was accused of partiality. A complaint was lodged against him before the President. NDA members along with five independent MLAs went to meet the President and complained against the governor and presented their stand. NDA also went to the Supreme Court on this issue. The Supreme Court ordered Shibu Soren to prove his majority on 11th March. Guruji had the belief that a few independent MLAs would support him and he would be able to prove majority but he understood that he did not have the majority and he resigned even before voting in the house. Later the Governor swore Arjun Munda in as the Chief Minister of the state. Five independent MLAs--Sudesh Mahto, Enos Ekka, Hari Narayan Rai, Chandra Prakash Chaudhary and Madhu Koda supported Arjun Munda instead of Guruji. Actually, Guruji failed to bring a couple of MLAs in his camp, hence he had to resign from the office.

He became the Chief Minister for the second Time in 2008.

Three days after Madhu Koda resigned from the post of Chief Minister i.e., on 27th August 2008 Guruji took oath as the chief minister for the second time. Once again it was the same governor – Syed Sibtey Razi. He swore Shibu Soren in. In 2005 also, Syed Sibte Razi was the governor who swore Shibu Soren in without checking for a mandate. A huge uproar occurred after that and Shibu Soren had to resign. Apart from one, all the ministers who took oath with Shibu Soren were the ones who were ministers in Madhu Koda government. Only Chandra Prakash Chaudhary was replaced by Aparna Sengupta. It meant that the team was the same as Madhu Koda's, only the leader had changed.

An independent MLA, Madhu Koda had been sitting in the chair of Chief Minister with the support of JMM, Congress and RJD. On 28th July 2008, Shibu Soren arrived in New Delhi and said "I want to do politics in Jharkhand and not in Delhi". His word was final. Shibu Soren had given this statement after a lot of calculations. It was because he knew what he had to do next. Therefore on 1st August 2008, Shibu Soren and Hemlal Murmu met Ahmed Patel, the political advisor to Sonia Gandhi and put forth his stand. On 12th August, UPA MPs in Delhi asked Madhu Koda to resign from the post of Chief Minister but Madhu Koda made it clear that he would not leave the post of Chief Minister. The dispute was bound to grow. On 17th August three ministers of JMM resigned from Madhu Koda's government. Later JMM sent a letter to the Governor, and withdrew their support from the government. After this, the Madhu Koda government was in minority. On 21st August Shibu Soren met Sonia Gandhi and Lalu Prasad and Madhu Koda was called to Delhi. He was asked to resign. After all this Madhu Koda was left with no other alternative but resign which he did on 24th August.

The meeting of UPA continued in Delhi. Congress had announced their support to Shibu Soren. Immediately after this, Lalu Prasad also came in his support. But despite all this, numbers were not adding up. Support of all the independent MLAs was necessary. Independents were united. They were supporting Madhu Koda and did not want a change in leadership at any cost. After Madhu Koda's resignation, slowly Shibu Soren built the atmosphere in his favour and started persuading the annoyed MLAs. He succeeded in this. Conditions of independent MLAs were agreed to and finally Shibu Soren became the

Chief Minister. Shibu Soren's government was running with the support from UPA. At that time Shibu Soren was not an MLA. He had to become an MLA within a span of six months from the day he became chief minister. He had to win an election prior to 27th February. For this Shibu Soren contested the election from Tamar seat but he lost from there. Results were announced on 8th February and there was not enough time left to contest an election from another seat to become an MLA. Therefore, he resigned. Shibu Soren could remain the chief minister for 4 months and 23 days only. What was most disheartening was that all those whom he had groomed and made MLAs either refused to vacate their seat or put unfavourable conditions. Shibu Soren was badly let down but there was nothing he could do.

He became the Chief Minister for the Third Time in 2009 again

After losing the MLA election from Tamar in 2009, Shibu Soren had to resign from the chief minister's office; but he did not have to wait for long to become Chief Minister again, i.e. for the third time. In the same year on 30th December Shibu Soren once again became the Chief Minister but this time the atmosphere had changed. No one could get a clear mandate. Earlier JMM used to be a part of the UPA. Shibu Soren was a two-time minister in the Manmohan Singh government at the centre but he changed his strategy after 2009 Jharkhand legislative assembly elections. He came along with the BJP. Shibu Soren came to power with the support of BJP, JDU and AJSU. His government had two deputy chief ministers – Raghubar Das from BJP and Sudesh Mahrto from AJSU. Raghubar was BJP state President and Sudesh Mahto was the chief of AJSU. Both were at the top position in their respective parties. BJP and JMM joining hands was a unique experiment in itself. What should have happened immediately after the formation of state actually happened nine years later. This government also did not run for long. BJP got angry because Shibu Soren voted against the NDA in parliament. On 24th May 2010 BJP withdrew its support from the Shibu Soren government. The government fell because it did not have the required numbers. Congress and Babulal Marandi's party JVM (P) also refused to support him. Shibu Soren tendered his resignation to Governor M O H Farook on 31st May. Thus, this time Shibu Soren was chief minister for five months only.

Voting against NDA Proved costly

Shibu Soren's government was running with the support of BJP, at that time he was an MP as well. On 27th April 2010 he had voted against the cut motion introduced by BJP. Angered by this, BJP withdrew its support from his government in the state. Although Shibu Soren wrote a letter to the then BJP president, Nitin Gadkari and expressed his grief for this mistake but BJP did not relent. Shibu Soren's letter to Gadkari was as follows –

Honorable Mr Gadkariji,

"It is brought to my notice that because of my vote on the cut motion brought by BJP in the parliament on 27th April 2010, BJP has withdrawn its support from the NDA government. You are aware that I have not been keeping well for the past few days. It was because of this that I committed the mistake. I want to assure you that JMM is fully with the NDA, and would continue to stick with it. I have struggled long for a separate state. My dream came true when the NDA government was formed at the centre. Now the time has come to realize those dreams. But the decision taken by the NDA has pained me. In order to save the situation from the bad governance of

Congress, NDA should reconsider its decision so that the current NDA government can continue on its path of development."

—Shibu Soren

Became Coal Minister at the Centre

JMM had contested the 2004 general elections with UPA. Manmohan Singh had inducted him in the cabinet and assigned him the workload of the coal ministry. But he could not remain the coal minister for long. In the mean time, the 30-year-old Chirudih massacre case had resurfaced. Huge pressure was mounted on Shibu Soren to resign from the ministry. Ruckus in the parliament started. Prime Minister Manmohan Singh was also under immense pressure. He asked Shibu Soren to resign. Then Shibu Soren went underground. It was not possible even for the Prime Minister to contact him. On 24th July 2004, Shibu Soren tendered his resignation to the Prime Minister through fax.

Became a minister in central cabinet once again

When he got bail in Chirudih massacre case in September 2004, UPA was continuously pressurized to once again induct him into the central cabinet.

JMM had organized the Parivartan rally in Ranchi on 28th November 2004. Just a day before the rally Shibu Soren was once again inducted in the Manmohan Singh cabinet where he was made the coal minister. A few months ago, Manmohan Singh had forced him to resign under pressure after the court declared him absconding in the Chirudih massacre case. But after four months Manmohan Singh was bound to take him back in his cabinet. One of the main reasons behind this was the 2005 Jharkhand state legislative assembly elections. This time also he had to quit the ministry for a different reason. Shibu Soren finally became the Chief Minister of Jharkhand.

Saved the Narsimha Rao Government

Shibu Soren has faced huge cases in courts several times and he has also been acquitted more than once. One of these cases was the case of taking money to save the Narsimha Rao government. This case became a talking point across the nation because a court had convicted former Prime Minister Narsimha Rao on the charges of bribing some MPs to gather support in favour of the government. Later Rao was acquitted from high court. The matter goes back to 1993. At that time Congress was in government at the centre and Narsimha Rao was the Prime Minister. A no confidence motion was brought against the government.

At that time JMM was not supporting the government but its four MPs, Shibu Soren, Suraj

Mandal, Shailendra Mahto and Simon Marandi voted against the no confidence motion and saved the government. Money was transferred to the accounts of MPs as well but it was not discussed anywhere. Almost two and half years later on 1st February 1996, the President of Rashtriya Mukti Morcha, Ravindra Kumar wrote a letter to the CBI informing about the issue and requested to investigate the matter. In his letter Ravindra Kumar explained that a money transaction has happened in lieu of supporting the Rao government. Narsimha Rao, Vidyacharan Shukla, R K Dhawan, Ajit Singh, Capt. Satish Sharma, Bhajan Lal, and Lalit Suri are involved in this conspiracy. Therefore, the CBI should investigate this matter and file a criminal case in this matter. When the CBI did not show any interest in this matter, Ravindra Kumar filed a public interest litigation in Delhi High Court and accused the CBI of not discharging its constitutional duty. Following this, the Delhi High Court issued a notice to the CBI.

Now this matter was highlighted and the CBI became fully active on it. On 25th March 1996, CBI filed a charge sheet against the four MPs of JMM in the court of the special judge Ajit Bharihoke. In the charge sheet it was mentioned that money was deposited in the accounts of these four MPs. On 5th September 1996, CBI arrested Shibu Soren, Suraj Mandal, Shailendra Mahto and Simon Marandi. A charge sheet was also filed against Narsimha Rao and six others in the month of October in the same year. It created a turmoil in Congress because Rao's name was also included in the charge sheet. Many other stalwarts of Congress were also trapped in this matter. On 3rd January 1997 Delhi High Court passed an order to release Shibu Soren, Suraj Mandal, Shailendra Mahto and Simon Marandi from Tihar jail on bail. Narsimha Rao, Satish Sharma, Veerappa Moily and other big leaders of Congress were given anticipatory bail. As the investigation carried on, new names cropped up. Buta Singh's name also came up and a charge sheet was filed against him also. Congress' worry was increasing because its big leaders were now being accused of corruption. Accusation was only one-- that payment of three and half crores was done to save the Narsimha Rao government. One of the accused, Shailendra Mahto turned approver on 17th March 1997 and pleaded for mercy as he had committed a mistake. He accepted that he received a payment of ₹ Fifty lakh.

After the hearing, Narsimha Rao and Buta Singh were convicted on 29th September 2000. It was the first occasion when a Prime Minister had been convicted in a case of corruption. A special court had given this ruling. Since the order was given by a special court therefore the doors of High Court and Supreme court were still open for the convicts. The only point of relief for them was that the court had ordered to seize the ₹ Fifty lakh given to Shailendra Mahto. Although Rao and Buta Singh were convicted but the quantum of punishment was still not decided, hence everybody was curious.

Three Years imprisonment each for Narsimha Rao and Buta Singh

The fateful day of 12th October 2000 also arrived. The special court sentenced Narsimha Rao and his associate Buta Singh to three years of rigorous imprisonment. They were also sentenced to pay a fine of Rs Two lakh each. It was the first occasion in the history of this country when a former Prime Minister was sentenced to imprisonment. The court also granted bail to the convicts in order to file petitions in a higher court. At the time when the judgement was being pronounced, the court room was filled. On the same day the court also ordered the CBI to file a case against Shibu Soren, Simon Marandi and Suraj Mandal once again. The court said that these three persons have misled the court when they said that bribe money was party's money. This matter should be reinvestigated. Since Shailendra Mahto had accepted his guilt and turned approver, court had already acquitted him.

Narsimha Rao and Buta Singh filed an appeal against the order of special court in Delhi High Court on 25th October 2000. The hearing went on for more than a year. On 15th March 2002, Justice R S Sodhi overturned the judgment of the special court and acquitted Narsimha Rao and Buta Singh. Later Shibu Soren, Simon Marandi and Suraj Mandal were also acquitted and it was stated that court can not interfere in matters that happened inside the parliament.

Shashinath Jha Case: From Life Imprisonment to Acquittal

Shibu Soren has spent his entire life in struggles and he has seen many ups and downs. He also went to prison several times during the period of agitation but there were some cases that almost broke him. One such case was the Shashinath Jha murder case. The Delhi court had sentenced him to life imprisonment in this matter. That day when he was sentenced to prison was one of the hardest days of his life. Although later High Court as well as Supreme Court had acquitted him in the Shashinath Jha murder case but the mental trauma that he had go through would have broken a common man for life.

Shashinath Jha was Shibu Soren's personal assistant. Guruji admired him very much.

Everything was going fine but one day a major incident happened. On 22nd May 1994 Shashinath Jha was kidnapped and on 24th May 194 he was murdered. Shashinath Jha's family accused Shibu Soren and his associates of his murder. They registered a complaint in a police station in Delhi. This matter was investigated by CBI. A human skeleton was found and CBI had said that this was Shashinath Jha's skeleton. In this matter CBI arrested Shailendra Bhattacharya, Nand Kishore Mehta, and Ajay Mehta from Ranchi on 13th August 1998. Accusations were made that in the parliamentarian bribery case Shashinath Jha had demanded his share from Shibu Soren. This aggravated the dispute and he was murdered. The CBI was already investigating this matter. On this order, Shibu Soren was arrested from his official residence in Delhi on 19th June 1998 and he was taken on 10 days remand. It was then the gravity of the matter was sensed. However, Shibu Soren was released on bail later. At that time the movement for separate Jharkhand state was also growing. Political activities had increased.

A separate Jharkhand state was also formed on 15th November 2000. On one hand these political activities were going on while on the other hand the Shashinath Jha murder was also being heard in court. In between all this Shibu Soren became the Chief Minister as well. He had to quit from the post of Chief Minister a few days later. Then he became the coal minister in central cabinet. During this time, the matter of Shibu Soren going underground in the Chirudih massacre had also come to the forefront. In 2004 general elections UPA government was formed at the centre. At that time JMM was a part of the UPA. Shibu Soren was inducted in the Manmohan Singh cabinet as the coal minister on 29th January 2006 but he could not remain in office for long. On 28th November 2006, the Tees Hazari court in Delhi convicted Shibu Soren in the Shashinath Jha murder case. As soon as the verdict came Shibu Soren was taken in custody and sent to Tihar jail. It was a big blow to Shibu Soren, JMM and UPA. Congress got the opportunity and immediately Manmohan Singh asked him to resign. On the same day Shibu Soren quit the office.

Now every eye was watching the court for the quantum of punishment. On 5th December 2006 Shibu Soren was sentenced to imprisonment for life with a fine of Rs Five lakh. Although CBI had asked for a capital punishment for him, Shibu Soren's advocate R K Anand requested the court to keep in mind his old age and service done for Jharkhand and award him minimum sentence.

It was the first instance when a central minister was sentenced to life imprisonment. Along with Guruji, his four associates were also awarded life imprisonment.

During the sentence hearing Guruji was very quiet and he was constantly looking at the ground. He did not talk to anyone. That day he spent four hours in court but remained quiet for the whole time. At that time Guruji was accompanied by Hemant Soren, several members of JMM and ministers. When the CBI counsel was demanding capital punishment for Guruji, even then he remained quiet. His face was expressionless. When the sentence was pronounced, Guruji's supporters were in tears. Some were even openly crying. Even before the sentence was pronounced, Lalu Prasad had said that Shibu Soren should resign on moral grounds. In this difficult time, Guruji was already abandoned by Congress. In this situation JMM leaders were standing with Guruji, especially Sudhir Mahto and Sunil Mahto. On the same night Hemant Soren declared that there was no need for Guruji to resign from the parliament.

Shibu Soren's opponents were constantly passing comments against him whereas his supporter and friends maintained that Shibu Soren can die but can't kill. He has been framed.

Guruji's old friends were standing by his side in these troubled times. An old and a long-time friend, comrade A K Roy said that Shibu Soren was afraid even to kill a mosquito. How can he kill someone? A K Roy had said that Guruji never believed in politics of murders therefore he had nothing to do with the murder of Shashinath Jha. After the judgment was pronounced, Guruji was sent to Tihar jail. He spent some time in Tihar jail. Later, he was brought to Jharkhand to appear in the Chirudih case hearing. He was kept in Dumka. When Shibu Soren was brought to Jharkhand, as soon as he alighted at Dhanbad station his eyes filled with tears when he saw his supporters. He also gathered self confidence which was evident on his face.

Guruji had appealed in the high court against his life imprisonment. The Bench of Justice R S Sodhi and Justice H R Malhotra in Delhi High Court cancelled the judgment of the lower court passed against Shibu Soren in the Shashinath Jha murder case. In addition to this, the court acquitted him due to lack of evidence. In its order, the court had said that CBI failed to produce ample evidence. After the order from the high court, Shibu Soren was released from Tihar jail. The CBI challenged this judgment from high court in the Supreme Court. On 27th April 2018, the Supreme Court passed its judgement and refused to interfere in the order passed by the High Court. The Delhi high court judement was in Guruji's favour. Thus, after a lengthy legal battle, Shibu Soren was acquited of all the charges in the Shashinath Jha murder case. On the day Guruji was acquitted, he spoke his mind and explained how CBI had framed him-how he was even sentenced to imprisonment for life. Finally, he got justice from the Supreme Court.

Chirudih Massacre: A 29-year old Matter Resurfaces

It is true that several violent incidents happened during the Jharkhand Movement. Shibu Soren carried on agitations against the elite class and the money lenders, and helped the tribal people get their land back. Several violent incidents occurred during this process. People died too. A confrontation between Shibu Soren's supporters and the elite was very common in those days. Bullets were fired from one side while the other side shot arrows. The Chirudih case was also one such case. After the formation of Jharkhand state, government had withdrawn most of the cases related to the movement but bad luck did not leave Shibu Soren here as well. All of a sudden The Chirudih case resurfaced in July 2004 and he was declared absconding. From streets to parliament, so much ruckus was created across the country that Shibu

Soren had to go underground and finally leave the coal ministry. Later, by the order of high court he had to surrender before the Jamtara court.

His opponents did not let Guruji, who fought a long and hard battle for Jharkhand, take a breathe of relief. It seemed as if he was born only to struggle. His luck ran out just when he needed it most. In the year 2000, when a separate Jharkhand state was formed, he could not become the Chief Minister, although it was not that he did not try hard enough. Gradually the general elections of 2004 also approached. Shibu Soren became a member

In people's court, just before his surrender in Chirudih case

of parliament from Dumka in these elections. Jharkhand Mukti Morcha was a part of UPA and after the formation of UPA government under the leadership of Manmohan Singh; Shibu Soren was later inducted in the central cabinet as the coal minister. Everything was going well. Amidst all this, on 13th July 2004, the Ranchi Express, a daily newspaper published from Ranchi carried an article that created a sensation across the country that Shibu Soren is absconding in a 29–year–old case. He has neither sought bail nor has he surrendered. The matter went back to 23rd January 1975. That day a chilling incident had happened in Chirudih.

A clash between the tribal and non tribal (these were either the elite or their supporters) people happened on that day in which more than 10 people were killed. Shibu Soren's name was not included in the FIR initially but was added later.

There were 69 accused in this matter out of which 59 had already appeared in the court but 10 did not. The case was being heard in the Sub-Divisional Judicial magistrate (SJM) court in Jamtara. That court had ordered Shibu Soren and other accused to surrender before 6th September 1986. That was the time of agitation. Police was looking for Shibu Soren in various other matters as well. Shibu Soren did not care and did not

Shibu Soren with Arjun Munda and other associates in JMM

surrender. This matter was buried since then and all of sudden in 2004 resurfaced like a ghost. In the mean time, no one had discussed this matter. This matter went back to 1975 and the situation had changed drastically since then. In 1980, Shibu Soren became a member of parliament for the first time. Since then, he regularly became an MP. He also became a minister in central cabinet and the chairman of Autonomous Council. He held meetings with the chief ministers, the prime minister as well other powerful allies but no one cared about this case. When the Chirudih case cropped up, NDA government was in Jharkhand and Arjun Munda was the chief minister. Arjun

Munda had replaced Babulal Marandi after a lot of hustle and bustle and political instability only a few days ago. Thus, as soon as this matter came up, Shibu Soren said that BJP's Arjun Munda and Babulal Marandi were behind this. He went on to the extent of saying that if he is a minister and an MP, how can he be absconding? BJP is framing him as a part of some conspiracy.

There is no debate regarding the fact that this matter cropped to settle political scores. Rivalry between Babulal Marandi and Shibu Soren goes back to long time ago. Both had been facing each other in elections as well and both have defeated each other at one time or another. In order to establish their hold in Santhal politics, both of them have come out against each other. Therefore, when the Chirudih matter came up Shibu Soren accused the BJP as Babulal Marandi had not left BJP and was an MP at that time. He was the national vice president of BJP as well. A faction of JMM was also targeting Arjun Munda for this as he was the chief minister. When the news was highlighted in the media Arjun Munda gave a statement that Shibu Soren is out on bail. After this he was accused of trying to save Shibu Soren. Chief Minister Arjun Munda was being targeted from both sides. One faction was accusing him of saving and the other faction targeted him for framing Shibu Soren. These accusations were not baseless. Arjun Munda had defected to BJP from JMM. Even though he had changed his political party but his personal relations with Guruji was very cordial.

Matter Raised in the Parliament

According to news reports, Shibu Soren was an absconder. JMM and Shibu Soren himself had strong reservations against the term absconder. Their argument was that if Shibu Soren was in public life contiunuously, had been an MP, a minister in the central cabinet, then why was he constantly called an absconder? Newspapers in Delhi also published this matter. After this, there was huge uproar in the parliament. NDA demanded the arrest of Shibu Soren. Arun Jaitley and Sushma Swaraj rased this issue in the Rajya Sabha and demanded resignation from Shibu Soren. Ultimately home minister Shivraj Patil had to issue a statement in the parliament on 17th July 2004 that Shibu Soren was neither a criminal nor an absconder because in 2003 court has taken back the warrant which was issued against him. Shivraj Patil clarified that whatever he is saying is on the basis of information furnished by the Jharkhand government.

Despite a statement from Shivraj Patil, this matter was not dying down. Those who had leaked this matter to the media were sitting quietly in a corner and enjoying the show. It was the UPA government and Shibu who were entrapped in this issue. Shibu Soren would have no idea even in his dreams that a matter from the days of Jharkhand agitation will prove so costly. On the other hand, NDA had a huge issue on its hands. Why would NDA let go of an opportunity to besiege the government that it had got due to Shibu Soren? When this ruckus was going on, Shibu Soren was not underground. He was regularly meeting tall leaders and clarifying his stand. In this process, he had met Shivraj Patil on 16th July. He was accompanied by Stephen Marandi and Sunil Mahto. It was after this particular meeting that Patil gave the clarifying statement. Till that time the fact that had come up was that the warrant issued against Shibu Soren was never served to him. Therefore, the SJM court reissued the warrant on 17th July 2004 so that no confusion remained.

It was no longer possible for UPA to stand in support of Shibu Soren. NDA's attack on the government was growing every day. Congress had understood that it was wiser to side itself from Shibu Soren otherwise the government may come in trouble. Therefore on 18th July 2004, Prime Minsiter Manmohan Singh pressurized Shibu Soren to resign. Shibu Soren had met the Prime Minister on that very day. In this process Manmohan Singh had made it very clear to Shibu Soren that if he is arrested then he must resign. If the politics in Delhi was in uproar then Jharkhand wasn't in peace either. Babulal had taken a very hard stance. He gave a statement that Shibu Soren is a criminal and he must prepare to go to jail. Arjun Munda was accused of saving Guruji but once the court issued a warrant against Shibu Soren, he too found a path to save himself. He said that the earlier warrant was not issued but now that has been done, the law will take its own course.

Warrant was pasted on his Delhi Residence

Jharkhand police received the warrant on 19th July 2004. From that day it became very difficult to meet Shibu Soren. Although he was still in Delhi and had met Lok Sabha speaker Somnath Chaterjee earlier in the day. Shibu Soren went to high court and through his counsel asked that if the warrant had been issued why wasn't it served till that day? On 20th July, the court declared Shibu Soren to be absconding. Now it was clear that after he has been declared absconding by the court, his troubles were bound to increase and he would not get any relief. He knew that police will do everything in its power to arrest him. Apart from this, now he could not move freely. He wanted to meet the leaders of UPA and present his stand before the police officials from Jharkhand could reach Delhi to serve the warrant.

Met the Prime Minister and presented his stand

The day the Jamtara court declared him absconding, Shibu Soren had actually gone to the parliament but did not take part in its proceedings. He met the prime minister and home minister and presented his stand in writing before them and explained how he was being framed in a political conspiracy. In his stand, he narrated the entire Chirudih case and the situation after that. By that time two officials from Jharkhand Police, Neeraj Sinha and Umesh Singh had arrived at his residence in Delhi. They could not find him there so the warrant was pasted at his residence.

When the police could not arrest Shibu Soren, there was an uproar in the parliament on the next day and a demand to present him was made. The chairman of the Rajya Sabha tried to calm down the members saying that Shibu Soren was on leave for three days.

Tendered his Resignation by fax

Shibu Soren was also planning his strategy. He knew that the matter belongs to the court hence the solution will also have to come from court. He had filed his petition in Jharkhand High Court but on 22nd July, Judge Laxman Oraon refused to hear his plea. The judge's argument was that in 1975 it was he who had penned down the statement from Lakhinder Soren, hence he can not hear the plea. Prime Minister Manmohan Singh had taken a tough stand by now. By 23rd July, even the prime minister was unable to establish contact with Shibu Soren. He had given clear orders to find the minister and take his resignation. Now there was no way out for Shibu Soren and he had already left Delhi. He knew police was looking for him therefore, on 24th July he sent his resignation through his son Hemant Soren via fax.

Hemant Soren, Hemlal Murmu, Teklal Mahto and Sunil Mahto took Guruji's resignation to the prime minister. By that time Shibu Soren had gone underground and it became extremely difficult for anyone to find him, meet him, or talk to him. Guruji had decided that he will remain underground until the high court passes an order. He would decide his next move only after any order from the high court. 26th July was the date scheduled for the hearing.

Meeting with Underground Guruji

I knew that it was very risky to meet Guruji and extremely difficult as well. I had good relations with other leaders of JMM also. Therefore, I was confident that if I tried I perhaps would gets a chance to talk to Guruji. Even after a lot of efforts, I was unable to contact Guruji's eldest son, Durga Soren. Other leaders had also switched off their phones. I knew that Sunil Mahto knew the whereabouts of Guruji. I had got the indication that Guruji was staying somewhere in Jharkhand. I stated my desire before Sunil Mahto, to meet and talk to Guruji for news before Sunil Mahto. I had cordial relations with Sunil Mahto and he also trusted me. I requested him to come along with me and fix a meeting with Guruji. Initially Sunil Mahto tried to brush me aside but later he agreed. He said 'I am giving you a vehicle; its driver will take you to Guruji." He was a new guy. "I had never met him. Sunil Mahto had

Shibu Soren chatting at an unknown location during his period of absconding

said that he can not accompany me as people in Jharkhand knew him and the police was tracking him as well. If he goes to any place, it will raise doubts with the police and this can put Guruji under risk. I agreed.

I was called to Kadma Ground in Jamshedpur. A car was waiting for me. I boarded it. After a journey of one and half to two hours I was in the village where Guruji was staying. That village was somewhere near the border of Jharkhand and West Bengal. It was a tribal majority village. Guruji had prior information about my arrival. He was dressed in a checkered kurta and pyjama and sat on a cot. He was dressed in the same clothes when he surrendered. He was completely calm. His face showed no tension. That village was far from the pakka road. None of those who surrounded him were known to me. None of those who were nearby carried any traditional weapon i.e., bow and arrow. Movement of people was also very limited at that place. It was staged as if everything was normal. There was neither any bike or car or jeep. Movement of vehicles would have raised doubts. I had a peaceful conversation with Guruji for over an hour. That day he had said "I am being framed. I am waiting for the order from High Court." He had said "You go and print it in the newspaper, wherever I am, I am safe. My supporters should not worry." I published the entire conversation in the 26th July edition of Prabhat Khabar.

Guruji had said 'I am not an absconder. Several times I won election from Dumka. I had been a member in the Parliament. I addressed more than a thousand meetings in these thirty years. I attended meetings in Jamtara as well, then how can I be an absconder? NDA got wiped out from Jharkhand so they had to do something to save their face. Shibu Soren is a revolutionist. He got a separate Jharkhand state for its people. He is not afraid of going to jail. I mulled many movements against the elite and exploiters. Many cases were filed against me during the movement. This matter is also one of those cases. Now I will decide only after tomorrow's judgment. The more the government troubles me, stronger the JMM will become. The government wants the state to burn and put the blame on Shibu Soren. The public is aware of everything. I have full faith in the judiciary and I respect the orders from judiciary completely. We have camped in Ranchi and taking forward the judicial process from there. Now the public will not have to wait for long. Whatever is destined to happen will happen soon. I have given clear instructions that even if the court orders are against me, under no circumstances should violence happen in the state."

His strategy was finalized on the day this conversation happened. I too got a hint of it. JMM had decided that if it comes to surrender in Jamtara court, a huge public meeting will be organized before that and around one lakh people will participate in it. This is what happened. The High Court reserved its order on 26th July. Now Shibu Soren had to remain underground for a few more days. Soon the day of 29th July arrived. The court ordered Shibu Soren to surrender before the Jamtara court by 2nd August. The court also cancelled the warrant issued by the lower court on 17th July and said that if Shibu Soren does not surrender before the court by 2nd August then the lower court is free to take any action. After the order from high court, it was clear that Shibu Soren had no other option but to surrender before the Jamtara court. Yes, there was a relief that he would not be arrested before 2nd August. It was so because the warrant had been cancelled.

As soon as the order from High Court came, Shibu Soren issued a statement that he will surrender before the Jamtara court on 2nd August. He did not reappear immediately because he was hiding and it would take some time to get to Ranchi from his hideout. On the next day, 30th July 2004, he appeared before the people in Ranchi. He was accompanied by Stephen Marandi and his eldest son Durga Soren. Guruji attacked BJP and said that BJP wants to turn Jharkhand into Gujarat. That day Guruji gave very interesting answers to the questions posed by reporters. One question was bound to come; where was he hiding? He answered "Where will I go? I was here only, among my people. I was explaining to them that we have to be patient." Very cleverly he did not reveal the name of the village he was hiding in. When he was asked "Guruji, how many cases are there against you"?. He answered "There is no record of it. When I was agitating against elitism, dozens of cases would be filed against me every day. There was shoot at sight order against me. Not only Piratand or Giridih, Chandankiyari, Navadih – everywhere cases were filed against me".

Now Guruji had time till 2nd August before he had to surrender. This meant that he had two days. On 1st August Guruji addressed a huge rally in Kanchanbera. He knew that if he does not get bail from the Jamtara court then he will have to go to jail. Therefore, he decided to go to people's court first. This has been the unique characteristic of Guruji. He delivers all the messages to the public directly. On 1st August, his supporters from Jharkhand as well as Bengal had come to listen to him. From the stage he repeated what he had said in Ranchi. To his supporters, Guruji had said that BJP wants to murder him inside the jail, they want to frame him. He is not an absconder. Why was this issue raised after thirty years? It is a political conspiracy. There also he repeated that he will surrender before the court on 2nd August.

On 2nd August 2004, Guruji surrendered before the court of additional district and session's judge in Jamtara. His bail plea was rejected and he was sent to 14 days of judicial custody. A camp jail was built for him in Jamtara women's college. He had to stay in jail for a few days. On 3rd September high court granted him conditional bail. A few conditions were put in front of him that he will appear in person on every date, he will not leave the country without prior permission from the court.

On 8th August Guruji came out of jail. This case went on. In between he was also put in RIMS in Ranchi for medical attention. Those days he remained very upset. He used to say "All my life I have struggled, now I am forced to stay inside.

I don't like it here." Till that time, he was not yet acquitted in the Shashinath Jha murder case. He was tense. Later the court acquitted him in Chirudih massacre case on 6th March 2008. Seven people were convicted in this case. Thus, after a long legal battle, the judgement from the court gave him some relief.

Binod Babu, A.K. Roy and Shibu Soren

Binod Bihari Mahto, A K Roy and Shibu had very cordial relations in the initial days. These three had come together to form the Jharkhand Mukti Morcha. When the first anniversary of formation

Shibu Soren, with his old friend A. K. Roy

was celebrated in 1973, the trio showcased immense power. Binod Babu and A K Roy were together since their days in CPM. Shibu Soren joined them later. It was Binod Babu who took the initiative. At that time Shibu Soren used to run the Sonot Santhal Samaj and Binod Babu was running the Shivaji Samaj. Both were social organizations and were organizing people to fight against social exploitations. One was organizing the tribal society while the other was organizing the Kurmi society. But away from these two, A K Roy was fighting the war for the cause of labours. Very soon they realized that they can continue the struggle together. A K Roy believed that red and green flags should be joined together to fight a battle against exploitations and mafia. Later the situations changed so much that A K Roy gradually distanced himself and carried on with his political career under the banner of MCC.

On the other hand, Binod Babu And Shibu Soren were still together but the ideological differences between them were very evident. Both of them participated in many movements near Tundi – Topachanchi and Dhanbad. Later Binod Babu was arrested under MISA and sent to Giridih jail. Binod Babu's arrest angered Shibu Soren so much that he encompassed Giridih city along with thousands of tribal people and raised the slogan – The doors of the prison will break and Binod Bihari will come out (jail ka fatak tootega, Binod Bihari chhootega), But later Shibu Soren's proximity with Congress increased. He surrendered during the emergency. At this point the distance between both of them began to increase. Shibu Soren lost the legislative assembly elections from Tundi in 1977. Shibu Soren believed that Binod Babu had a role to play in this. Once again Shibu Soren joined hands with the Congress for the 1980 Bihar state legislative assembly elections. Binod Babu was against this. In the same election, Congress fielded its candidate against Binod Babu as well. Binod Babu got angry due to this.

The ideological difference between them kept on increasing. Binod Babu formed another organization. After this a special meeting was called and President of the organization, Binod Bihari Mahto was expelled from the party. In 1984, Shibu Soren made Nirmal Mahto the President of Jharkhand Mukti Morcha.

Although they had ideological differences, Shibu Soren had immense respect for Binod Babu and always addressed him as Babu. Binod Babu died in 1991. After that a magazine, 'Binod Stuti' was launched in his memory. What Shibu Soren wrote in that magazine displayed the kind of cordial relations he had with Binod Babu. Guruji wrote –

Father of Jharkhand, Binod Babu

Political relations with any person are based on the level of practicality but when this relation reaches the dimension of trust and respect then its significance becomes a social treasure. Late Binod Babu was like a father figure to me. He always bestowed his unconditional and pure love on me as if I were his child. He was the starting point of the story of my political life and in his last days he became the symbol of greatness for me. Binod Babu was the father of Jharkhand and founder of Jharkhand Mukti Morcha. I remember in the 1970s when I used to live in Jainamore. During that time Sonot Santhal Samaj and Shivaji Samaj,

Shibu Soren, with Binod Bihari Mahto

both social organizations had achieved a powerful structure and strong base. The huge population of Jharkhand was standing behind it with full devotion and waiting for a call to give everything it had. During such a decisive time, it was Binod Babu who advised a fusion of these two organizations. As a result, a strong political organization in the name of Jharkhand Mukti Morcha arose. At that time, in the backdrop of preparation for the movement for Jharkhand, we had to take along social movements such as not letting the tribals drink, stopping the elite class from exploiting the poor tribals, make them literate, etc. From 1972 to 1974 both political and social movements went along side by side. From 1972 to 1982, Binod Babu and I carried on our political struggle together. We separated because of ideological differences. This happened in order to serve his personal ambitions. The paratrooper leader tried to take advantage of his mass base and communist inclination. Despite these differences, in 1989 once again we came together on common issues. In my political life we were like father and son. He was the one who helped my entry into politics and who had shaped my role in politics. Thus, even today I call him father.

This tribute by Shibu Soren displayes the amount of respect he had for Binod Babu.

Similarly, even though Guruji and A K Roy had chosen to move on different paths, but when Guruji was caught in troubles and his name cropped up in case of murder, A K Roy was standing strong by his side. A K Roy had said very clearly that Shibu Soren could not do such a thing. When Roy Sahib was caught with illness then one day Shibu Soren went to meet him at his house and they both joked a lot. They got lost in old memories. The picture tells the story that both were talking to each other freely. Such was the relation between them.

Guruji Considered Nirmal Mahto His Brother

Shibu Soren and Nirmal Mahto had always enjoyed very cordial relations. Guruji had always considered Nirmal Mahto to be his younger brother and addressed him as Nirmal Babu. Nirmal Mahto was also around six years younger to Guruji. After their mutual, introduction they were together for a very short span of time. But within that short span, they both turned Jharkhand Mukti Morcha into the pioneer political party of Jharkhand. Nirmal Mahto joined Jharkhand Mukti Morcha in 1980 and was assassinated only seven years later in August 1987. Nirmal Mahto completed the journey of becoming the Party President from a mere worker in these seven years only. It was a very big achievement. At that time Shibu Soren was the General Secretary (Central Committee) of

Shibu Soren with Nirmal Mahto in a programme

Jharkhand Mukti Morcha. Nirmal Mahto mainly did his politics in Singhbhum whereas Shibu Soren's work field included Dhanbad, Giridih, Hazaribagh, Santhal Pargana and areas near Ranchi. Politics in Jharkhand saw a major shift after the Guva firing incident on 8th September 1980. Jharkhand Mukti Morcha was successful in increasing its mass base in Singhbhum after that. In those days Nirmal Mahto was associated with N E Horo's Jharkhand party but he was recognized as someone who fought against the money-lenders and exploiters. In those days, the poor class in Jamshedpur was much troubled by the moneylenders. Nirmal Mahto used to stand against those moneylenders. He used to hit those moneylenders with his belt. Those who understand Shibu Soren's style of politics know very well that he plays his cards very close to his chest and he makes his strategies in his mind. His vision was working in pushing Nirmal Mahto forward as well. He had recognized Nirmal Mahto's power very early and was aware that someday he will need him by his side.

In the initial days Binod Babu held the position of president while Shibu Soren was the general secretary in Jharkhand Mukti Morcha. But on several occasions ideological differences between them surfaced up in the open. Although the ideological differences cropped during emergency but even after that, this difference surfaced again in 1980 when Shibu Soren decided to join hands with Congress. Binod Babu was against this. Therefore, it was evident that it was not possible for them to continue together for long. The politics of Jharkhand Mukti Morcha was founded on two strong pillars – tribal and Kurmi. The organization derived its power form these two societies. Therefore Shibu Soren knew that in order to take JMM forward he would need support of a powerful Kurmi leader who could replace Binod Babu. Binod Babu and Shibu Soren had immense mutual respect for each other and this is the reason Shibu Soren never criticized Binod Babu in public.

One of the bases of Nirmal Mahto's joining hands with Shibu Soren or JMM was the Guva firing case. An incident of police firing took place in Guva on 8th September 1980 in which 11 tribal people lost their lives. Bhuvaneshwar Mahto was arrested in that case but the police was looking for Shailendra Mahto and Bahadur Oraon. In the mean time it was decided that a huge meeting against police firing should be organized in Chaibasa. Shibu Soren, A K Roy and Binod Babu were also invited to that meeting. Scheduled on 28th October 1980. Shailendra Mahto was given the responsibility of printing the pamphlets for this meeting. Shailendra came to Jamshedpur from Chakaradharpur. He met Nirmal Mahto and sought his assistance in printing the pamphlets. This was the first face to face meeting between Nirmal Mahto and Shailendra Mahto, although, they had heard about one another. At that time, despite being in Jharkhand Party, Nirmal Mahto helped Shailendra Mahto in printing the pamphlets. Shailendra Mahto stayed in Nirmal Mahto's house for 2–3 days. During this period, relations between them grew more cordial. Later the pamphlets got distributed and the meeting also happened. Nirmal Mahto regularly took updates about this. Now he was getting inclined towards JMM. After Durga Puja, Nirmal Mahto along with Shailendra Mahto and a few other friends visited Hazaribagh jail. There he met the Kolhan revolutionaries who were in prison. At that time Nirmal Mahto felt JMM was a party of his liking.

In between all this, in 1980, Nirmal Mahto while addressing a meeting of labours in Adityapur (near Jamshedpur) announced that he had joined Jharkhand Mukti Morcha. This announcement was widely welcomed. It was a blow to the Jharkhand Party. Till that time Nirmal Mahto and Shibu Soren had not met each other. Their first meeting took place on 20th February 1980, when Shibu Soren had gone to address a meeting of temporary labourers of Tata Steel who were on a strike in Jamshedpur. After that meeting Nirmal Mahto became more active. Guruji also realized that Nirmal Mahto had the potential to carry the party forward. Therefore, he gradually increased Nirmal Mahto's responsibilities. Initially he was elected the president of district JMM in Singhbhum.

In the mean time on 21st October 1982, an incident of police firing took place in Tiruldih. Two students of Chandil College, Ajay Mahto and Dhananajay Mahto were killed in that incident. The fear of police was such that no villager was ready to take the bodies of the dead students back to their village after the postmortem. When Nirmal Mahto came to know about this, he took upon himself the responsibility to complete this task. He himself went along with the dead bodies, and their last rites were performed in front of him. Shibu Soren came to know about this incident and this impressed him a lot. JMM's first party convention was organized on 1–2 January in Saraidhela in Dhanbad. In this conference Nirmal Mahto was appointed a member of the central working committee of the party. Now Nirmal Mahto's area of work expanded from Singhbhum to entire Jharkhand. In the mean time differences between Binod Babu and Shibu had been rising a lot. A meeting of JMM's central working committee was called on 6th April 1984 in Bokaro and on the recommendation of Shibu Soren Binod Babu was replaced by Nirmal Mahto as the party President. It was a very big responsibility. This was an example of the amount of trust that Shibu Soren placed in Nirmal Mahto. Within three and half years Nirmal Mahto had reached the top most rungs of the party.

Nirmal Mahto became the party president for the second time

Second party convention of JMM was held in Ranchi from 26th to 28th April 1986. Once again

Nirmal Mahto was elected as the president central committee. Shibu Soren remained the general secretary. In 1984 itself, Shibu Soren could have made Nirmal Mahto the general secretary and himself the party president if he had wanted to do so, but he pushed Nirmal Mahto forward. Now the pair of these two expanded the movement very swiftly. In the mean time, the AJSU was founded as well. Shibu Soren wanted Nirmal Mahto to become a member of legislative assembly or the parliament. Therefore, he fielded him (Nirmal Mahto) from Ranchi in the 1984 elections but he lost and stood fifth. After the assassination of Indira Gandhi, the wind was blowing in Congress' favour and not only Nirmal Mahto but even Shibu Soren (Dumka) and Shailendra Mahto (Jamshedpur) lost the elections. In the 1985 legislative elections he fielded Nirmal Mahto from Ichagarh because he had done a lot of work in the area. But unfortunately, Nirmal Mahto lost that election as well and secured the second place. Nirmal Mahto himself was never interested in becoming an MLA or MP. It was Shibu Soren's wish that Nirmal Mahto wins an election. One day Shibu Soren had said to Nirmal Mahto – "Nirmal Babu, you never speak for yourself. One seat in the MLC has gone vacant. You file the nomination, victory is assured." But even after a lot of persuasions, Nirmal Mahto did not agree and in his place made Chatrapati Shahi Munda MLC. Such were the relations between Nirmal Mahto and Shibu Soren.

Wound Marks on the body

Once both Nirmal Mahto and Shibu Soren had gone to attend a JMM programme at Jamtara. It was winter, and both were shirtless and basking in the sun. Suddenly Guruji asked him

Grief-stricken Shibu Soren attending last rites of Nirmal Mahto after his martyrdom

"Nirmal Babu there are too many wound marks on your body. Where did they come from?" To this Nirmal Mahto replied that once he suffered a near fatal attack. He was hit with iron rods all over his body. He was seriously injured. The attackers thought he was dead and had left him there. Later, somehow he was saved. The attack was so intense that deep wound marks were all over his back. Those wounds did not heal acompletely even after so many years.

Wept on the assassination of Nirmal Mahto

Everything was going fine and suddenly on 8th August 1987 Nirmal Mahto was shot at and assassinated in front of Chamariya guest house in Jamshedpur. When Shibu Soren got the news, he reached Jamshedpur immediately and wept profusely over Nirmal Mahto's dead body. At that time, members of AJSU were in anger and wanted revenge. Shibu Soren knew that millions would gather for Nirmal Mahto's last journey, therefore he announced that last rites will be performed on 10th August. Some incidents of violence were happening in areas near Jamshedpur therefore police wanted the last rites to happen as soon as possible. They put pressure for this and were met with resistance.

Nirmal Mahto's last rites were carried out on 10th August. For the entire period, Shibu Soren stayed with Nirmal Mahto's dead body. A condolence meet was organized just before the last rites. Addressing the meet Shibu Soren had said that Nirmal Babu had sacrificed his life for Jharkhand and we could not let it go to waste. And with this, with a heavy heart Shibu Soren and JMM workers paid their tributes to Nirmal Mahto.

Gyan Ranjan and Shibu Soren

Shibu Soren and Congress leader Gyan Ranjan had very cordial family relations. Congress also kept benefittting from this relation. It was during the legislative elections in 1980 when Jharkhand Mukti Morcha and Congress joined hands for electoral politics. The credit for this goes entirely to Gyan Ranjan. The erstwhile Prime Minister Indira Gandhi had recognized Shibu Soren's potential. She also understood that if the Congress party wants to become stronger in south Bihar and garner tribal votes then it must join hands with Shibu Soren and his party Jharkhand Mukti Morcha. If someone can persuade Shibu Soren for this then it can only be Gyan Ranjan. Therefore at Indira's behest, Gyan Ranjan talked to Shibu Soren and persuaded him. After this, he took Shibu to Delhi where he fixed his meeting with Indira Gandhi. An agreement was achieved for the legislative assembly elections. At that time there were two camps INC Bihar politics. One camp was of Kedar Pandey while the other belonged to Jagannath Mishra. Gyan Ranjan was considered to be a part of the Kedar Pandey camp while Kartik Oraon was close to Dr Jagannath Mishra. First round of talks between Shibu Soren and Gyan Ranjan had the consent of Kedar Pandey. It was agreed that JMM will contest on 45 seats but as soon as Dr Jagannath Mishra came to know about this, he raised an objection. He tried to persuade Indira Gandhi by saying that if Congress leaves so many seats for JMM, its mass base will decrease in the area. It can be dangerous in future. After this, the seats for JMM in the alliance were reduced to 25. Although an alliance was achieved, but it was yet to become an on ground reality. Violating the alliance, both Congress and JMM fielded their candidates on seats they desired. Congress (I) fielded their candidate even against Binod Bihari Mahto (JMM president) in Tundi. JMM contested for 31 seats and won 11 (eleven).

Shibu Soren had become an MP prior to the legislative elections. In the year 1980, Shibu

Soren contested as an independent candidate and became a member of parliament from Dumka. Congress was worried about south Bihar since a long time. Jaipal Singh's Jharkhand party was very renowned in this tribal majority area. After Jaipal Singh joined Congress in 1963, it was assumed that the voter base of Congress will increase but it did not happen. Therefore, Indira Gandhi wanted that Shibu Soren shoud be befriended in order to increase its influence among tribal voters. This job was given to Gyan Ranjan. Both Gyan Ranjan and Shibu Soren had immense respect for each other. Both knew each other already. Gyan Ranjan's relative was a teacher in Gola and Shibu Soren's father was also a teacher in Gola; both met every day. Whenever Gyan Ranjan visited his relative in Gola, he met Shibu Soren (who was very young at that time). Both knew each other since those days. After that period Gyan Ranjan spent most of his time in Ranchi while Shibu Soren launched a movement against the elites and went to the jungles. When Shibu Soren surrendered in 1975, it was Gyan Ranjan who had advised him to do so. Despite being a member of Congress party, Gyan Ranjan was a staunch supporter of a separate Jharkhand state and used to attend meetings as well. Once, Shibu Soren had also attended Gyan Ranjan's rally in Ranchi. Whenever Shibu

Soren came to Ranchi, he used to stay at Gyan Ranjan's residence. At that time Gyan Ranjan was unmarried and his mother used to cook food for Shibu Soren and his associates. Guruji used to stay at Gyan Ranjan's house for many days at a stretch and wherever he had to go he went by Gyan Ranjan's car. Such was the relation between them. In the mean time, if needed, they used to meet at night only.

Once there was by-election in Banka. Congress had appointed Gyan Ranjan to stop Shibu Soren from holding meetings in Banka at any cost. He had to be stopped. Shibu Soren wanted to go to Banka. Gyan Ranjan, Shibu Soren and Suraj Mandal along with a few journalists (Hariom Gupt, Avinash Thakur and Shafique Ansari) started from Ranchi to go to Banka. Gyan Ranjan kept delaying the journey on purpose. The journey of one day took four days to complete. Shibu Soren was aware of this but he had lot of respect for Gyan Ranjan and did not say a word. Recalling that journey, Avinash Thakur says "On the fourth day we reached Banka and directly went to the hotel Shibu Soren did not hold any meeting in Banka."

Shibu Soren also benefitted from his relations with Gyan Ranjan. D N Sahay, a senior police official was very close to Gyan Ranjan. Whenever Guruji was in trouble, he talked to Gyan Ranjan. D N Sahay's help was always available. Both Gyan Ranjan and Shibu Soren did not let this relation grow weak.

Old Friends' Companionship in Troubled Times

It has been a characteristic of Shibu Soren that he always developed personal relations with his friends. There are many people who have not met him for years but the affection has not withered with time. When he meets someone even after several years, by a quick reminder he digs out old memories with them. Therefore whenever Guruji was surrounded by troubles, such people always came out and stood by his side. A K Roy and journalist Satish Chandra are among such people. These two were people who knew him for a long time. You should read what they had written.

We are proud of that Movement: A K Roy

History has a rule. Power does not come to those who struggle. Even if it does, it does not come according to his wishes. It is true for Shibu Soren as well. When the anti Jharkhand forces lost to Soren, they have played this move. It is not an attack only on Shibu Soren but on every comrade, who is associated with the Jharkhand movement. Jharkhand is not Nagaland, but do government and courts function like this only? Action should be taken against him who raised this case. This case itself is a crime. The High Court should penalize those officials. JMM was formed in 1973 in Dhanbad, a huge rally took place that was presided by journalist Mukutdhari Singh. Was he a tribal? Is JMM a party only for tribals? The backdrop of Shibu Soren's struggle is also associated with the red flag. Even the name of the party was borrowed from Vietnam struggle. In Vietnam also the the party that was struggling was called Vietnam Liberation Front. The English translation of Jharkhand Mukti Morcha is Jharkhand Liberation Front. The battle for a separate Jharkhand was fought in a new style from 1970 and it was led by Jharkhand Mukti Morcha. We are proud of that battle. Shibu did not kill anyone, hence he should not apologise. If he has to go to prison, he should go. This has raised his stature and will continue rising. People will ask all the questions. Even from the judiciary. Do the poor get justice in this scenario? The matter of Chirudih was also related to the Jharkhand Movement. Why did the government not revoke that case? Those who never contributed to the movement, in fact tried to derail it, are the same people who are doing this to sabotage the movement even today. It is a crime against Jharkhand.

How did the drum (maander) beat, why did it go silent?

When Shibu Soren was facing attacks from all fronts in the Chirudih massacre case, at that time journalist Satish Chandra, who was very close to him, wrote his opinion on the entire episode. Satish Chandra had known Shibu Soren for a long time. Therefore, he wrote his opinion without any malice. It was also published in a leading daily in 2004. Read below Satish Chandra's opinion

I am an eye witness of Shibu Soren's journey from his entry in public life till today. Shibu Soren was as well—known name in Tundi and surrounding areas in 1970. His movement against money–lending, elitism, bribery, alcoholism and other social evils had a huge resonance. It was for the first time that an amazing organization had formed by the coming together of all the villagers including the tribals. The entry of government officials was also prohibited in the villages. Shibu believed that these government officials had always exploited the tribals and villagers--registering their lands in someone else's name, eating their goats and chickens, and ask for bribes. Therefore, they should not be allowed to enter the villages.

Whenever the government officials, moneylenders or elite class people tried to enter the village or did some mischief, dugdugi was beaten to raise the alarm. All the villagers rush together and chased away the exploiters. Government officials had actually stopped coming to the villages. The sub inspector of Topachanchi, Ghatak had accepted the challenge and tried to enter the village, he was killed there. The hero of that incident was Binod Bihari Mahto but the name that was dishonoured was of Shibu Soren. Shibu Soren had done a huge social revolution. But due to his terror neither the villagers went to towns nor did the people from town come to villages.

In 1974, K B Saxena was appointed the deputy commissioner of Dhanbad. He recognized the potential of Shibu Soren and tried to bring him to the main stream. Under heavy security he took me along with him, 50 kilometers away from the town - in village Palma. It was my first meeting with Shibu Soren. We had talks, formulated the next strategies. Then suddenly the mafias got Saxena transferred. Laxman Shukla replaced him as the deputy commissioner of Dhanbad. He had already worked in Dhanbad earlier and knew everybody.

He continued the efforts to bring Shibu Soren into the main-stream. But he had many cases against him and it was impossible to bring him out in the forefront without getting him bailed out. I was the one who bailed him.

I was very impressed by his social revolution. I conducted his first interview in 1975 that I got published in Dinman, Aryavart and Indian Nation. Along with renowned social servant, Gaurishankar Agrawal, I went to him and presented a sewing machine, lantern and some books. Till 1990, Soren continued to work like an ideal solitaire and friar. His fame had spread all across Jharkhand. In the mean time, Suraj Mandal joined him after getting trained from Sanjay Gandhi's Youth Congress and very soon became his close confidante. In 1990, JMM secured probably six seats in the Lok Sabha and twenty in the Bihar legislative assembly on the slogan of a separate Jharkhand state. That same year Samresh Singh tempted the owner of Valley refractory, Bajrang Agrawal, with a Rajya Sabha seat and assured him all the votes of Jharkhand Mukti Morcha. Although Bajrang Agrawal lost but his 40 lakh rupees were spent. Who took how much, no body knows. But after that every MLA from JMM became owner of Maruti cars.

In 1990, Lalu Yadav became the chief minister of Bihar. JMM had raised the slogan of a separate

Jharkhand state. Lalu Yadav declared that a separate Jharkhand would be possible only over his dead body. All the residents of Jharkhand were taken aback when a separate Jharkhand was not formed, but Suraj Mandal became the undeclared prince of South Bihar. He was considered the chief minister of south Bihar. But Suraj Mandal always put Shibu Soren on the front and like Bharat, started ruling south Bihar on behalf of Ram's shoe (Kharaun). Frustrated by the greed of Suraj Mandal, Lalu Yadav said "Out of 100 Suraj gives 1 rupee to Shibu Soren and keeps the remaining 99 for himself." After that Suraj Mandal was replaced by Krishna Mardi. Still Suraj Mandal continued to do his politics under the shadows of Shibu Soren. When the Jharkhand Area Autonomous Council was formed, Shibu Soren became its Chairman but the name proposed for deputy chairmanship was of Gautam Sagar Rana. Shibu Soren stuck his name out and made Suraj Mandal the deputy chairman. That council too had become a hub of looting. Finally, Shibu Soren got frustrated with Suraj Mandal. In the mean time, Shibu Soren's eldest son Durga Soren had also become a leader and an MLA. One scabbard cannot hold two swords. Suraj Mandal was sidelined. But having lived with him for a long time Suraj Mandal was aware of darkest secrets of Shibu Soren. The Chirudih case, due to which Shibu Soren had to resign, was known only to Mandal. I was a journalist and very close to Guruji, yet I did not know about that case. Others also do not remember such long-forgotten cases. But when Shibu Soren still not take Mandal back, he dug up this case only 15 – 20 days ago and took his revenge by forcing Guruji to resign. Whose luck will favour or run out in politics, nobody knows. But for now, the Suraj did bring Shibu's star down.

Shibu Soren and Prohibition

Since the beginning of his movement against the elite class, Shibu Soren had been an advocate of prohibition. He himself had never touched alcohol in his entire life. When he joined the movement after the murder of his father, Shibu Soren had decided that not only will he free the poor from the clutches of elite class, but prohibit alcohol as well. He had understood the fact that the elite always used alcohol to usurp the lands from the poor, and exploited the tribal women. The main reason behind the poor situation of the tribals was their bad habit of drinking. Shibu Soren formed the Tribal Reform Committee (Adivasi Sudhar Samiti) in order to remove the social evils prevalent in tribal society. The chief objective of this committee was to raise public consciousness in the tribal society and keep them away from alcohol.

In an interview given in 2003 Shibu Soren had said “I was going crazy. I felt like killing all the elites, but how many could I kill? Then, there was police behind these elites. Gradually I started the struggle. I continued to struggle for the elite agitation and prohibition. People had started to trust me. Thousands would gather on my single call. When I told them about prohibition some villagers would start to oppose me. Once I beat my own uncle with a stick for drinking. Uncle was sitting near the stove. Our argument about his drinking was going on. When I hit him with the stick he fell down. Other members in the house thought he fell due to inebriation. Later he quit drinking. People from the village only started saying that he is working against our culture. The boy has turned Christian. But still, I continued my struggle against alcohol. I always had the tendency to run away. I left my home to find a job in Bokaro. There I saw that tribal people worked very hard during the day and by evening they used to drink and fall. Their women were physically molested by contractors and people who came from outside. I could not bear to see all of this. I raised my voice against them as well."

This opinion of Shibu Soren shows that he was well aware of the ill effects of alcohol. That is why in his youth itself he started a movement against alcohol.

When Guruji took refuge in the hills of Parasnath, struggled in Tundi and began the social reform and development work from the ashram in Pokhariya, he always held prohibition at top priority. In those days he used to run a parallel government in Tundi. Guruji had made a rule that anybody caught drinking would be beaten. He too used to beat the alcoholics. Used to practice Delhi road (a way to punish) also. The effect of all this was that many villages in which he had resonance became alcohol free. Even after that, whenever he got a platform Shibu Soren never failed to raise his voice against alcohol.

When Jharkhand Mukti Morcha celebrated its first foundation ceremony in Dhanbad on 4th February 1973, Shibu Soren introduced many resolutions. Prohibition was also one of those. Prohibition was also discussed in first party convention of Jharkhand Mukti Morcha in Dhanbad on 1 and 2 January 1983. At that time,

Shibu Soren was the General Secretary Central Committee of JMM. Nirmal Mahto also used to run a movement against the alcohol mafia even before he joined JMM.

Shibu Soren had arrived Ranchi in order to participate in the Intellectual conference in 1978. It was a huge programme. Speaking in that programme, Shibu Soren said "the government also has a role in breaking a society. I will give you two examples. First is alcohol. Societies are broken; because of alcohol, evil has entered. Government distributed alcohol licences and taught people to drink. Whatever little money they earn after a hard days labour, the government and businessmen dealing in alcohol rob it from them. Not only this, people have been dragged into situations where they are forced to sell their lands. Alcohol has ruined the society. Alcohol is the root cause of quarrels in homes; it is the root of divide in society.'

How strongly Guruji considered alcohol as the biggest barrier in the growth of tribal society can be understood from the fact that in 1980 when he entered the parliament for the first time, he raised the issue of alcohol in his first speech. At that time he was only 36 years old. In the parliament he said "I am tribal, was born in a tribal family. We have seen that the government is unable to address the cause of our weakness. Our society is in tatters. The rich and landlords supply alcohol to us and grab our lands. Not only this, they have also raped us. At a the places across the country where harijans and tribals reside, alcohol shops should be shut down."

In 1981, when Guruji got an opportunity to write an article in Dharmyug, he explained about the ill effects of alcohol. He wrote "tribals have another bad habbit. We had asked the Bihar government to shut down alcohol shops in tribal localities, but our demands were not met. Contractors cater alcohol to them and exploit them. The same situation prevails in West Bengal. Government had distributed abundant alcohol licenses to Marxist workers in tribal areas. They are also exploiting the tribals in Bankura."

All these incidents can explain that Shibu Soren has always opposed alcohol and intoxicants. JMM has also passed resolutions in its general conference, but it is also true that three times he became chief minister of Jharkhand but his government never took a decision on prohibition.

It is possible that government generates revenue from alcohol and no government would want to close its source of revenue but it is also true that alcohol has ruined many families.

Shibu Soren has Always Spoken Frankly

Shibu Soren has given interviews or written articles in the papers and magazines of the country from time to time. These interviews and article are very important in order to understand him, his ideology and views. Shibu Soren has always been accused of being against the outsider (dikus), but when we read his views and interviews, he presents a very different face, especially after the formation of Jharkhand. Even though his views might appear hard on certain issues in order to attain political mileage but there real meaning is very different. Some of his selected interviews are as follows.

I am a born communist

Question: What has Jharkhand Mukti Morcha done for tribals?

Answer: If I speak frankly then we have helped the tribals regain their lands that were usurped by the landlords. Even more important than this is that we have successfully returned the self respect of tribals. Now they are not ashamed of being a tribal. One should never forget that for all these years the tribals have led a life of slavery. It is not easy to overcome this mindset psychologically.

Question: Till now how much land has been reclaimed by the tribal with your help?

Answer: Lots of land, but at present it is not possible for me to give the data.

Question: Why did you decide to become an MP? How did it help your movement?

Answer: My life was always under threat. Now (after becoming a parliamentarian) the government will have to be more vigilant. Even after this, if someone wants to send (me) to jail, who can stop them. As a parliamentarian I won't be able to give my people anything, I have told them. I shall always speak the truth.

Question: What has been the stand of other parties regarding your movement?

Answer: Every party, be it Congress, opposition parties or the communists, they have always treated us with distrust. I have been called a foreign agent and what not. I have told my companions – trust yourself and not me.

Question: Is it true that there are differences between you and A K Roy of the MCC?

Answer: If I am wrong people will not support me. If A K Roy is wrong then people will not spare him either.

Question: But is it true?

Answer: We have fought the battle together. It will continue in future as well. There are differences only between the workers of two parties.

Question: How far are you from your goal of a separate Jharkhand?

Answer: I don't know if a separate Jharkhand will be formed in my lifetime or not. My goal is to awaken the people *(Published in Probe India in March 1984).*

I am Ready for a Fair Referendum

Question: Recently, central home minister Buta Singh has given a call for talks on problems of Jharkhand region. What is your take on this?

Answer: I am glad that central home minister has proposed to talk on the problems of Jharkhand region. I consider it the first step in the success of our movement that ultimately the government has agreed that there are problems in the region which need to be addressed. Whenever I am invited for the talks, I will gladly go.

Question: Will you give priority to any one of your demands in these talks?

Answer: The government shows expense of crores of rupees in this region but no actual work is done. Therefore, now people of the region have strong belief that unless this region gets the status of a separate state and someone from this region is allowed to rule it, it is impossible to either understand or solve the problems of the people. Therefore, whenever the talks happen, our primary demand will definitely be a separate state of Jharkhand.

Question: The central government has already made it clear that no demand for a separate Jharkhand state will be entertained. How do you plan to persist on the demand for a separate Jharkhand?

Answer: Government's thoughts and statements can be correct in their own capacity, but it is still too early to say what will be the direction of these talks. But we strongly believe that our problems can not be solved unless we get a separate state.

Question: If the percentage of representatives from this region in Bihar legislative assembly is increased, don't you think that will force the government to pay more heed to the problems of this region?

Answer: That too won't solve the problem.

Question: Shall we understand then that you do not trust the elected representatives of Indian National Congress?

Answer: Absolutely, I do not trust them. What will happen with that, if the legislators of the Indian National Congress instead of raising the issues of people of this region are busy in becoming the yes-men of ministers and chief minister. Only those people from the region are made ministers who can just remain yes men. Examples of Indranath Bhagat and Bhukhla Bhagat are in front-of us. One replaced the other as minister, but what has happened? Even earlier, many tall tribal leaders have been made ministers but the system is such that nothing could be done.

Question: Those legislators from the Indian National Congress who support your demand for separate state, do you trust them or not?

Answer: We have absolutely no trust in them. Today they are demanding, tomorrow they will get some position and forget about those demands. We have past experience of this.

Question: Even if the central government accepts your demands and agrees for the formation of a separate state. What kind of rule system would you give priority to for this region?

Answer: Whatever the democractic system will be, we will accept that only. Nothing like Nagaland or Mizoram, where non-Naga or Non–Mizo people cannot be a part of the government. Whoever resides here—tribal, non tribal or minority has a complete right to contest the elections and represent the people.

Question: You have been demanding a separate Jharkhand for so long now, but does it not seem that you don't have the expected support of the people of this region in this?

Answer: Support is there, and every resident here seems a supportor of my views. He too feels that this region cannot get justice unless a separate state is formed.

Question: If that is true then why don't you get much success in elections? At present you only have 11 MLAs, that too from two divisions.

Answer: Number of MLAs is no parameter in the present system. Here the stamp is not put by people themselves but someone else does it for them.

Question: If, during the talks, the central government puts forth the proposal of a referendum for the formation or not formation of Jharkhand?

Answer: If the referendum is done in a fair manner and without any meddling by the Bihar government, then I will accept it any day. If the referendum is done by central government using its own machinery, then I am sure most of the people will support a separate Jharkhand.

Question: If the regional people do not support your demand in this referendum, then what will you do?

Answer: Then I will let go of my demand. If the people do not come along then who shall I demand it for?

Question: In the recent turn of events, don't you think that the mantle of this movement is shifting to the younger generation from the old?

Answer: This is the achievement of our movement and organizational structure that more and more young people are joining our organization and are getting ready to lead the command, where on the other hand people form organizations, carry them on their shoulders, life long and die.

Question: If the Jharkhand movement goes in the hands of young people, will it remain peaceful?

Answer: We will make it peaceful.

Question: If the government does not accept your demands, what will you do ultimately?

Answer: It is possible that in helplessness, local public gets angry and situation explodes.

Question: What stand will Jharkhand Mukti Morcha take in that condition?

Answer: At the outset, Jharkhand Mukti Morcha will stop the mineral resources of the region from going out to other states. It will cripple the entire nation's economy. We will compel the government to agree to our demands.

Question: Will the government let that happen?

Answer: How many people can the government kill? People of Jharkhand never shy away from either killing or being killed. In addition to this, Jharkhand Mukti Morcha will train people about their rights so that corrupt government officials can–not exploit them due to lack of knowledge. Only those officials who bring good policies will be able to live here. We will create such an environment. Santhal Pargana is an example of this. The terror of the rich and moneylenders that prevailed in the region is now gone. No one can even think of usurping tribal lands by fraud or force. *(Prabhat Khabar, 17th November 1986)*

Our Struggle is a the exploiters, not the outsiders

Question: There is an accusation against you that you carry the politics of Congress inside JMM.

Answer: This accusation has been levelled against me by those who want to do my character assassination. Actually, it is the wrong—doing of a few corrupt Congressmen, a few petty leaders from other leaders and beureaucrats. After Jaipal Singh, the strongest movement in Chhotanagpur is going on in my leadership. The selfish group of this movement is hellbound on defaming me. This bad mouthing against me is being done by the same people.

Question: What is the relation between AJSU and JMM?

Answer: We only had formed AJSU. Our objective behind this was that the students could get political training so that they can give capable leadership to the people.

Question: Is AJSU running according to your plans?

Answer: A few unwanted elements had entered the organization. Activities of such people was under suspicion. These people had started working at their own whims without consultation from the organization or central committee.

Question: How do you want to fight the battle for Jharkhand? Whom do you consider the outsiders?

Answer: We want to fight the battle for Jharkhand under a democratic set up and according to the constitution. We want that a separate state should be formed where we can be heard and our problems are addressed. After past years' experience, all our hopes have been shattered. Now our exploitation cannot end until a separate state is formed. When people begin to lose faith in democratic state, violence emerges. Central and state governments get maximum revenue from Jharkhand region. They take our resources and in return level different accusations against us only. We are being attacked because of our demand for Jharkhand. Our demand started in the decade of the 50s. After that, several states have been formed on the basis of language, culture, caste and many other things. Punjab, Haryana, Goa, Mizoram etc., are a few examples. On the contrary, our forests became the centre of exploitations. Road were constructed to carry logs from the jungles. After the logs were carried out and jungles were destroyed, those roads disappeared. Government is not at all concerned about those roads any more. Forest guards of the jungle say that the jungle belongs to them. The tribals say that it has belonged to us for thousands of years. Police has colluded with the contractors and jungle officials. Therefore, a confrontation is a very natural course.

We consider people who have a tendency to trouble (dik) others as outsiders (diku). Even our man can be a trouble maker. Non tribals are not outsiders. Thousands of non tribals are committed to Jharkhand. When the exploiters are attacked, they do a bad publicity that outsiders are being chased away so that the character and objective of the movement can be maligned.

Question: Students of AJSU have demanded that the tribal MLAs and MPs should resign. What are you doing? Can this struggle turn violent?

Answer: We in the party had reconsidered the advantages of becoming an MLA or MP? It used to occur in my mind that if nothing substantial is being done then we should resign. Officials are corrupt, nobody is willing to listen, but such matters will ultimately be decided in the central working committee. People from AJSU have given this call to establish their own name. There are some MLAs who are supporting this call from AJSU but are not resigning themselves. People behind AJSU are not good. Culturally, we pick up the bow and arrow since the time of birth. We cleared the jungles and claimed it by the use of bows and arrows. At that time wild animals used to attack us. Now new people have captured the jungles. We oppose the inhuman torture done to us by contractors and corrupt officials by using bows and arrows. We don't have bombs, pistols or army. We don't want the atmosphere in Jharkhand to turn violent but the government is unable to understand this. Contractors of different programmes, contractors of Swarnrekha, contractors of Tata – all of them are robbing us. We do the manual labour of carrying bricks and stone in various programmes and for the contractors while they loot all the money. These contractors harbour criminals, molest our women and deny us the minimum wage. Our two workers are imprisoned for the past two years under National Securities Act for asking minimum wage. People of Jharkhand are raging due to this atmosphere. In addition to this, the police also trouble us. In Ranchi, Jamshedpur and Hazaribagh, the same station in-charge is sitting in the same police station for the last ten years. They threaten and rob us of our money and exploit the tribals. Actually, these station in-charges are the centre of terror and exploitation. What is more surprising is that they are even more powerful and resourceful than the superintendent of police. Their masters who are sitting in Patna, openly help them. Fifty lakh people from Chhotanagpur have gone to other places in search of livelihood. Just think about it, people from outside come here and exploit us while we roam here and there in search of livelihood; sell our dignity. In reality, police station, court and market everywhere we are being exploited. *(Ravivar, December 1987).*

AJSU has done foolishness

President of Jharkhand Mukti Morcha, Shibu Soren is a combative leader. He has seen many ups and downs from the start of the movement till today, and has also seen a lot of things. Now, he has given a new turn when he formed Jharkhand Vananchal Morcha along with members of Vananchal camp of Bharatiya Janta Party. Read below an exclusive conversation with Shibu Soren on important points of the movement and his alliance with Bharatiya Janta Party–

Question: How did the Jharkhand Mukti Morcha form an alliance with Bharatiya Janta Party all of a sudden?

Answer: The alliance is definitely all of a sudden, but the necessity was being felt for a long time. There should be a separate state, everybody should have equal rights, and this is the fundamental point.

Question: It has come to notice that on 13 districts agreement has not been reached?

Answer: We had never given our consent for 13 districts. BJP wants a Vananchal comprising of 13 districts. We are still firm on our demand for a separate Jharkhand.

Question: Then what is this alliance?

Answer: The alliance is done in order to struggle for a separate state together. If the mandate comes for 13 districts, then that is what will happen.

Question: Will there be an alliance with BJP for elections or not?

Answer: We will decide that later.

Question: BJP had sent a proposal form AJSU through Pravin Singh. Is this not the reason behind the initiative from JMM?

Answer: Your information cannot be completely wrong. By declining BJP's proposal AJSU has shown its foolishness. It is the desire of the people of the region. Public also want the same. Therefore, we will continue the movement together. Jharkhand Coordination Committee is behind all the failures of AJSU.

Question: Why do you have such views for the Jharkhand Coordination Committee?

Answer: Do you know what Jharkhand Coordination Committee is? In Jharkhand, the coordination committee faction is the dance team while the other faction plays the drum. Similarly, there is a third faction is for the development of regional languages. Jharkhand Coordination Committee is formed by joining these factions. They are only doing drama in the name of politics.

Question: What are the points of differences?

Answer: Even if there are differences, JMM has no role in it. I must tell you that JMM had presented a detailed programme for the distribution of seats among Jharkhandi parties prior to parliamentary elections. My proposal was – with the consensus, AJSU should get 2 seats, Binod Bihari Mahto, Jharkhand Party and Jharkhand Kranti Dal gets 1 seat each. Jharkhand Mukti Morcha asked for 7 seats. Despite this an alliance could not be formed.

Question: What was the reason that the alliance could not happen?

Answer: The reason is shallow pride of the leaders. Horo Sahib wants all the seats of Jharkhand. AJSU was thinking about this but they have not yet decided anything. You can presume that every party wanted more seats than their potential. I had claimed it back then and still claim that if we fight the elections together then Jharkhand candidates will be victorious on more than a dozen seats. Today we have a dozen MLAs and three MPs. The situation of other parties of Jharkhand is also before you.

Question: Union minister of state for home affairs, Subodh Kant Sahay has recently held talks with leaders of AJSU. On the other hand, JMM has been kept out of this. What could possibly be the reason behind this?

Answer: Boys of AJSU are very gullible. In Rajiv Gandhi's time, Buta Singh had betrayed now Subodh Kant has laid this trap.

Question: What kind of trap?

Answer: Subodh Kant has shown a sign of trickery by calling the leaders of AJSU to Delhi. You should know that when the boys of AJSU went to Delhi, Commissioner of Chhotanagpur, Chandan Basu brought Dr Munda and B P Kesari to meet me. I refused to go to Delhi for talks. Later remaining people fled to Delhi. You must be aware of what happened in Delhi.

Question: Recently a big faction of Muslims has left Congress to join JMM. What is the reason behind this success?

Answer: Adivasi, Sadan and Musalman, these are the three pillars of Jharkhand. Till now Congress had kept Muslims in the dark. Muslim–minds were filled with hatred towards the non-Muslim communities. Now people have begun to realize the truth. They know that Jharkhand Movement is not exclusive. In Assam, Muslims are being victimized in the name of movement. Every–where Muslims are victimized but they are treated with equality in Jharkhand. Now Jharkhand Mukti Morcha is getting support of different Muslim organizations across the nation.

Question: Till when will you support the National Front?

Answer: We have given our support to the National Front because we are all against Congress. If the government will–not agree to our demands, we can withdraw our support as well, but this will be decided in JMM first.

Question: Are there any chances of alliance with Jhakhandi parties if mid—term elections happen?

Answer: The doors of Jharkhand Mukti Morcha are always open but I am against those who desire more than what they deserve. I am also aware of who is capable of what. If some–one desires more than their capabilities, alliance is not possible.

Question: Talks about alliance were going on before the legislative assembly elections as well, but it did not happen.

Answer: Like I said earlier, people talk about

alliance but desire more than they deserve. Horo Sahib wants entire Jharkhand. The list given by AJSU contained those seats that we had already won. The remaining people had the same attitude. I had said to Horo sahab - you should contest only in those places where your chances of winning are high. We were even giving tickets to boys of AJSU. The only condition was we will decide the seats. If the boys of AJSU had listened to us they would have had 10 MLAs. Shibu Soren would have done everything in his power to ensure their victory. If Besra is an MLA today, it is because of us. It is my challenge that JMM would have made atleast 60 MLAs. But the lions of Jharkhand Coordination Committee ruined everything. These people neither want to contest elections themselves nor are they in favour of others contesting. I am ready to step down from the post of President of Jharkhand Mukti Morcha for Jharkhand. I had proposed we should all come together to run Jharkhand Mukti Morcha. I requested to Horo sahab as well, you are most senior amongst us, you should become the President. I will be a worker but Horo sahab is still stuck in the past. His argument is 'my party is the oldest party, how can I wrap it?' The question was never about the party, nor is it today. People are running the business of politics. Those who deserved the mandate got it. Now people are repenting. There is still time, a lot can still be done.

Question: How is Lalu Yadav's government functioning?

Answer: Exactly as it should.

Question: In order to solve the matter of Jharkhand, Subodh Kant Sahay is waiting for a report from concerned states. Lalu Yadav's government has also sought time. What will you do after time lapses?

Answer: I will not decide anything on my own. Shailendra Mahto, Suraj Mandal and other will decide collectively.

Question: What have you decided for the future?

Answer: Our only objective is a separate Jharkhand state. We will continue the struggle until we get a separate Jharkhand (Prabhat Kahabar 5th August 1990).

Where Should the Tribal People Go?

—Shibu Soren

Tendency to exploit, and a step motherly attitude towards the tribal has been the practice since the beginning and now they are frustrated with this. It is in the backdrop of this fundamental issue of exploitation that we are demanding a separate Jharkhand state. We waited patiently that some one will think of us, but now this possibility seems bleak. Although even after the formation of separate Jharkhand state, there is no guarantee that our economic condition will be better. Our leadership can also turn brokers. Therefore, it is our call to continue the struggle against injustice and exploitation. Today the biggest reasons behind the exploitation of tribal people are the system of contractors and tradesmen. In the British era and even today these people enjoy sweet terms with the administration. In 1957, these tradesmen murdered my father. He was killed for speaking the truth. As a result of this, we could not study but the tradesmen were still there. He had other people as well. System is also with them. Therefore, we started to unite against them. Now our objective is to build a state that is free of exploitations. This is the demand of people, a democratic demand. Non tribal people, tribal people all are in support.

Tribal people do not belong to any caste. They are those who have been living here since the beginning of time. Therefore, we have the first claim on this country but today we are the most backward. Chhotanagpur Santhal Pargana is the most resourceful region of India. Still, its people are hungry and unemployed. The biggest reason for this is the reckless cutting of the forest. For centuries, tribal people have lived only in those places where forests are found in abundance. In the forests, a tribal had every thing to eat - fruits, vegetables etc. but today the government is cutting those forests and planting artificial forests. Sagwan and eucalyptus are being planted. The main objective behind this is to make furniture available for the rich in town, but we don't sleep on furniture. This is why the tribal people have also launched a movement against this deforestation.

Shibu Soren, with Dr. Ramdayal Munda

Contractors of the forest pay 1 – 2 rupees to the tribal people and get the forest cut. Then, when the land is surfaced, the forest department says that this is government land and the tribal will have to move out. The tribal packs his home and has moves out. Then after a few days the same situation arises in the new place. Afterall, where should the tribal people go?

But after creating such a situation, the government officials of Bihar government say – nothing can happen without our orders. What laws were framed in independent India, I don't know. This is how the administration challenges the tribal people. Therefore, our fight is with the government officials and not the non tribal residents who live here. The atmosphere of tension between dikus and tribal people is being created on purpose. Government is not promoting education in tribal regions. Today illiteracy is our biggest weakness. In order to promote education, we have opened many night schools. There are a few people in tribal region who think that if the children of tribal people get educated then who will do their work? Christian missionaries have done a lot of work in the field of education. I myself do not follow christanity but I appraise the feeling of sacrifice in them.

A lot of effort is also made to create a rift between non-Christian and Christian tribal people so that the divide among us remains but poverty knows no religion. A poor is poor and all he needs is food. Tribal people have one more evil. We asked the Bihar government to not allocate alcohol contracts in tribal region but our demand was not given consideration. Contractors cater alcohol and exploit them. A similar situation prevails in West Bengal as well. Government has issued licences to Marxist workers in abundance in tribal region. They are also exploiting tribal in Bankura district. Therefore, we want to say, whoever is in the government, our welfare is not possible until we govern ourselves.

(Shibu Soren had written this article in special edition of Dharmyug, Adivasi Asantosh, published on 30th August 1981).

Matter of Jharkhand's Society, Culture and Development of Education

In the process of working for the Jharkhand movement Shibu Soren (Guruji) continued leading it directly from the forests and on the streets. The Jharkhand movement garnered support even from the intellectual class. During the entire movement, intellectuals had given immense support, organized conferences and seminars, wrote articles, and gave their views to take the movement forward. In the process, whenever any organization, party or institution organized intellectual programs for Jharkhand movement, they always had complete assistance from Shibu Soren. He used to attend these programs and keep his views. In 1975 Shibu Soren surrendered and came out of jungles. Three years later i.e. in 1978 biggest program on Jharkhand movement was organized in G E L church compound on 6th and 7th May. Editor of Shaalpatra, Vir Bharat Talwar was the organizer. It was an amazing conference that was attended by intellectuals from across the country. Revolutionaries were also called in this program. Shibu Soren had also attended this program himself and put his views forward. He did not say a single word about the separate Jharkhand state; he motivated the people to strenghthen the society, strenghthen their culture, quit alcohol and focus on education. In that program Guruji appeared in the role of a socialist and a social reformist. Reading this speech gives an insight of Guruji's dream. Here is an excerpt from what he said in 1978.

Today it is for the first time that a program of intellectuals from Jharkhand is being organized. It is a matter of extreme pride and pleasure. Looking at this strengthens my faith in the bright future of Jharkhand. I am no intellectual. Whatever I have experienced living with the people of Jharkhand and their life struggles, on that basis I shall put my views in front of you. What I have understood is that in order to make the people of Jharkhand prosperous, strong and unified, for the development of Jharkhand and for the contribution of Jharkhand in development of India it is necessary that the society of Jharkhand should be strenghthened. Jharkhand's culture should be developed according to historical traditions and every effort should be made to educate the people of Jharkhand. I would like to speak a few words based on my experience in this regard. You are wise people; you understand history, sociology culture and education. You should examine my words and debate in the backdrop of history and prepare such program and policy on the points of society, culture and education that might be accessible to the people of Jharkhand, that has resonance with the dreams and aspirations of the Jharkhand and works for their development; that can show them the way forward.

People of various communities reside in Jharkhand. For example Santhal, Munda, Ho, Oraon, Kharia, Kurmi, Sadan, Hindu, Musalman etc. Out of these a few societies mingle a lot while few don't. For example, Santhal and Munda mingle well but Santhal and Oraon don't. But it is also true that in all these societies there exists a unity which we can call as 'Jharkhandi Unity.'All these societies have their own social organizations and social rules. For example, a Brahmin is not needed to solemnize a marriage in Jharkhandi societies.

Organizations of our societies used to be very strong earlier. People were bound by the rules of societies and organizations. Like a village head in Santhali society is addressed as' Manjhi Gomke.' The head of entire region is called 'Dishum parganait.' People were kept unified using them as a medium. Today cracks in these organizations have led to weakening of the social fabric. But in regard on my Santhali brotherhood, I can claim that it still has the potential that can still reunify the society.

When a few people from outside came here with Brahaminism ideology and tried to forcefully impose their concept of high class – low class on people of this region, started the custom of temples, priest, mode of worship etc, then the Santhali people did flee in jitter but they did not surrender their own society to Brahaminism. This is the reason our Santhal society which is based on equality is still intact. Even today our tribal society exhibits a live example of socialism. For example, hunting in the jungle and equal distribution of the catch among everybody, from dogs to humans. Our traditions, goodness, unity and self respect is still intact. This is the key to our future.

Today, a few boys of our societies have got education and they have gone to high posts but how has this benefitted our society? After getting education, they forget their responsibilities towards the society. They get influenced by the dazzle of bad culture of other rich people and let alone the matter of development of their culture; they forget their own language and culture and even start attacking them. Many boys go to schools and colleges and marry girls from other societies and leave their own people. Why does this happen? It is so because our social organizations have weakened, its boundations and rule have been weakened. If our organizations are strenghthened and the rules are strictly implemented on its people then these educated lads will stand only with the society, will think about the betterment of society and use the education they received as a result of struggle of the society for the development of society.

When our society was united then there was no divide of high and low in the society. Everybody in the society was equal. We never hurt each other. Everybody used to work together. Even the government has played a role in breaking our society. I will give two examples here. First is alcohol. Societies are broken because of alcohol, evil has entered. Government distributed alcohol licences and taught people to drink. Whatever little money earn after hard days labour, government and alcohol businessmen rob it from them. Not only this, people have been dragged into situations where they are forced to sell their lands. Alcohol has ruined the society. Alcohol is the root cause of quarrels in homes; it is the root of divide in society.

Second example is jungle. Economy of a society and social organizations are deeply correlated. Earlier this region was filled with jungles. A tribal used to get six months ration from the jungle itself. Rains poured in for cultivation and the erosion of soil was stopped. The social economy was self dependent. In these conditions they stayed together and adhered to one social organization and its rules. The tribals were attacked. Their jungles were usurped, were sold to contractors in auction, jungles were ruined and its wood were cut and sold. Their economy was ruined. This harmed the agriculture as well. Dry seasons increased. People started to scatter and flee. People started to become slave of contractors for pennies. They started drinking, left their parents, left their wives and kids. They went far far away. Society was breaking.

The Sal trees have been cut to such an extent that it cannot grow anymore. In order to strengthen the social organization we must stop alcohol, we must stop deforestation. All these should be stopped atleast for next twenty years. Until a society is clean and strong, it cannot do anything for the country. Last month, a conference of the All India Santhal Society was organized in Asansol. There we took a few steps in order to strenghthen the organizations of society. A uniformity was brought in different names of societies. Belief of considering drinking alcohol and hooch in festivals as a part religious tradition was negated. We urged the government to consider the rules of Santhali marriage and heredity as laws. Rules were formulated for marriages outside the society. Days were fixed for celebration of festivals like baha erak, navai sakrat etc, it was decided to build jaherthan or manjhithan just lke temples and mosques. Many other decisions to fortify the society were also taken.

It is my view that all the societies of Jharkhand should get organized, only then will we able to something in an organized and disciplined manner. History tells us that in order to enslave any society, its culture is attacked. We have been facing attacks since the time Eklavya's thumb was cut off. We have always thwarted these attacks like we learnt to use two fingers instead of thumb to shoot arrows from the bow. In order to strenghthen our society, it is very important to preserve and nurture our culture. There are many MLAs and MPs who go to Patna – Delhi and get entrapped in the evil of foreign liquour and other cultures. They forget their own culture and traditions. What good can they do for Jharkhand?

In order to promote our songs and dances cultural council and cultural programs should be done. Our girls will dance in the villages for sure but they will have to stop dancing in fairs and other places. This is promoting corruption. If there is respect for our societies our youth will get less attracted towards the dazzling clothes. Now let us come to the point of education. Our rulers have always deprived us, the working class of education because they know that if we get educated, we will break the shackles of slavery and stand on our feet. Therefore, Brahmins made a rule that Shudras can not read Vedas. It is still visible today that landlords and tradesmen do not let the schools be built.

Wherever schools were opened in village areas they too proved to be a sham. If there is a building for school there is no teacher, if there is a teacher, the building is not. If there are both, the teacher does not teach. If he teaches, students don't understand what he's teaching because he is a man of a different language. Moving forward, this education is such, in which students learn to exploit, to discriminate, they don't learn to do good to others. This system of education is such in which a man learns to hate to earn money from produce and love to earn money from fraud. This education is such due to which our boys break the society and leave the society. This is why people say that what will my child do with this education, he will become useless.

But education is important for our development. Till date no government or intellectual from Jharkhand has been able to show a path for the development of education. Today, we need a correct education system. We must impart such an education which helps us grow, our culture and society lasts and nurtures. Our children put their heart in production, learn to love the people and do something for the good of people. We must persuade those who run from education. The habit to study should be inculcated from childhood. For this, night schools are very helpful. Wherever you might be in the day, in the night sit beside a lantern and do study something. One who is educated it is his duty to arrange for a lantern that is a group of boys to study. Everybody should get such education in schools as well as colleges. Simply relying on the government won't work. We have to put the efforts ourselves if we want the development of education. Promotion of education should become a movement.

I will now rest my voice. You are educated, intellectuals. With all your support we can definitely achieve all these. This is my dream, my aspiration.

Thank you.

Watchful Against the Enemies' Conspiracy Against the Jharkhand Movement

In 1978, first serious effort was made to speed up the Jharkhand movement and include group of intellectuals in it. A message was given out through these conferences that the Jharkhand movement did not belong to a particular group but the entire population that lived in the region of Jharkhand. Those days the matter of insider and outsider had also cropped up. It was also propagated that it was a movement of the Christians. Shibu Soren had himself written a piece in magazine, Jharkhand Varta (edition 3rd June 1978) and cautioned people by putting forth his views. Guruji had given a very clear message. His article is still has the same relevance for the furure of politics even today after the formation of Jharkhand as much as it was in 1978. Given below is the article written by Guruji.

Today the people of Congress, Indira Congress, adhering to the ideology of Jana Sangh inside the Janta party are conspiring to malign the Jharkhand movement, create divide in it in the name of religion, by running poisonous campaign in the name of insider and outsider and by creating riots. Enemies of the Jharkhandi people have published false news in the news paper that in the procession of Jharkhand movement in Ranchi slogan to break the temple and mosque, connect yourself with the church and quit Chhotanagpur (mandir masjid todo, girijaghar se nata jodo, chhotanagpur chhodo) were raised. It is beingly wrongly propagated that the Jharkhand movement is the movement of Christians. Rumours are being spread that after the formation of Jharkhand, all the outsiders will be forced to leave.

Since the ruling class is not getting success in crushing or trampling the demand for just right, the movement for a separate state by 3 crore exploited people therefore they want to wreck this movement through falsehood and poison of communalism, but they will not be successful in their nefarious agenda. No power in the world can now break the unity of the people of Jharkhand or their movement for rights. In Jharkhand, only 10 percent are the followers of Christanity. Out of remaining 90 percent, apart from 5 percent brokers, the remaining 85 percent are the followers of different religions. Similarly, the Jharkhand movement is the movement of 95 percent people which is comprised of Christans, Hindus, different tribals, Muslims and Sikhs – followers of all the religions. Today out of all the leaders of Jharkhand movement, the maximum are non Christians. N E Horo, Justin Richard, Moses Gudiya, Binod Bihari Mahto, I i.e. Shibu Soren, Bagun Sumbrui, Kartik Oraon, Vasant Narayan Singh, Devendra Manjhi, D C Murmu, Haricharan Sinku, Sohan Lal Aneja, A K Rai, Anil Kumar Sinha, Satyadev Sahu, Jahur Ali, Biseshwar Prasad Kesari etc. are the leaders of the Jharkhand movement. Out of these leaders of the Jharkhand movement, apart from the first three, every one else is a non-Christian. Does this fact about the Jharkhand movment and its leaders not prove that this propagation by the enemy that the movement for Jharkhand is a Christian movement is a white lie? The truth is that Jharkhand movement is not a movement of any religion. It is a political movement by the people of Jharkhand for their democratic rights. There is no chance of any one religion in it, but the conspiracy of the enemy is that he brings out the question of any one religion so that the other religion stands up against it. This way they wish to derail the political movement for the region of Jharkhand.

In Jharkhand, the attempt to spew venom in the name of Christians and non Christians is done by same set of reactionary and communal people who have spread communal riots all across the nation. People know them very well. These people cry about Indian culture and make long speeches about national unity and integrity but they create rifts among people of different cultures and different castes among various religions so that the exploitative rule of capitalists and imperialists can continue; so that the poor continue to fight among themselves and the strong can continue to trample upon the weak. These reactionary and communal forces do not want the people of Jharkhand to have their own state. This is why they are plotting a conspiracy and the newspapers of the capitalists are helping them. What is this conspiracy? Just give it a thought. They provoke the tribal people to beat and chase away the non tribal and to the non tribal they say that after the formation of Jharkhand non tribal people will chase you out. They call the tribal Hindus and field them against the Christians, then they go to the hindus and tell them that tribal people are not hindus and create a rift between them. They field the Kurmis against the Manjhis and

Manjhis against the Kurmis. They provoke the Hindus against the Muslims and tell the Muslims that the Christians are against you. Those who have plotted Hindu-Muslim riots all along their life, today want the Hindus and Muslims to unite against the Christians. Then they create rift of castism and forward and backward among the Hindus. Such dishonest and corrupt people go and tell one thing to the people of one religion and one caste and then they go to the other religion and caste and tell them the exact opposite. The people of Jharkhand should clearly identify these enemies of the movement and then whoever tries to propagate these lies, they should get hold of him and award severe punishment so that no one dares to repeat it.

Similarly, there is another lie that is propagated – after the formation of Jharkhand, the outsiders will be forced to leave. We have busted this lie earlier also and once again want to say out loud that no one will have to leave after the formation of Jharkhand. The movement of Jharkhand is not about keeping or chasing anyone. The movement is entirely for the cause that the people of this region get their own state and the people of this region work for its development. Programs should be made according to the necessities of the region and its people make their own agenda for development.

The wealth of this region is used for raising the standard of life of its people. This movement is a struggle for political rights and the right to self determination of the people. This movement has nothing to do with the question of insiders or outsiders. The very question of insider and outsider is wrong. After the formation, Jharkhand will be remain a part of India and people of every other state or region will have the same rights to come here, stay here, work here as that of the local people.

Shibu Soren's First Speech in the Parliament

Shibu Soren became an MP for the first time in 1980. He had won the election from Dumka Lok Sabha seat. He got a chance to speak in the parliament for the first time when the parliament was discussing the tribal–harijan report. Many stalwarts had participated in that debate. His first speech itself was very impressive. Other parliamentarians had very carefully listened to his speech. In his first speech itself, Shibu Soren had discussed all those issues which he had been fighting for a long time. He had raised the issue of tradesmen and exploitation of tribal–harijan as well as prohibition. His first speech in the parliament states—

Honorable Speaker Sir,

You gave me an opportunity to speak on the 25th report related to harijans and tribals, I thank you for that. Many friends here said a lot of things about their problems. I want to say something in few words only. As far as the problems of harijans and tribals are concerned, even thirty years after the independence they are the same as earlier. We had raised a movement against the exploitation by the tradesmen in Bihar, south Bihar, Santhal Pargana and Chhotanagpur. These kinds of report have regularly been published – in the name of welfare of harijans and tribals, in the name of their land security. But they were not benefitted in any district. We fought a battle of our rights. We were always lebelled as rebels and communists but we did not care about that and compelled the government to bow down and took our lands back. The weakness and illness that we have, should be taken care of. I am a tribal born in the house of a tribal. We have seen that the government is not capable of addressing our weakness. Our society is in tatters. Tradesmen and landlords cater us alcohol and take our lands. Not only this, they were also robbed of their dignity. The battle for land is growing everyday. Government has made laws to return the land but the lands are being snatched away. Therefore, concrete steps should be taken in this direction. Such officials should be sent to work among the harijans and tribals who have an interest to work among them. For the welfare of harijans, problems related to their lands must be solved. Wherever harijans and tribal people live, in any part of the country – alcohol shops should be shut in those parts. We are dependent on jungles. We are born there, in the jungles, harijans, tribals and poor people of the jungle lead their lives in the jungles. Those jungles have been ruined after government rules. We demand that these jungles are not ruined but that they are saved. Around eight or ten years ago I raised a movement for land in Chhotanagpur Santhal Pargana region for which I was slapped with false cases. I would like those cases be revoked. Our culture is getting ruined and the government should look into this matter. If our culture is ruined, we will be ruined. We have raised a movement and demanded that the tribal people from Bihar, Chhotanagpur, Santhal Pargana want to form a separate state of Jharkhand.

In addition to the parliament speech, there were several occasions when Shibu Soren gave historical speeches in various public meetings. We are putting forth a few of his speeches so that you are able to understand the circumstances in those days and Shibu Soren's views on them.

Date 15th March 1992 Place: Ranchi

Patience is now Running Out

Addressing a historic public meeting in Morabadi ground in Ranchi, Shibu Soren had said if the need arises all our MLAs and MPs will resign from their positions and if required pick up arms as well and will snatch a separate Jharkhand state. Now our patience has run out and the agitation scheduled from 21st March will be decisive. That agitation will decide the kind of mandate we have and how we take a separate state. In the Jharkhand Bandh of 21st March and economic blockade from 22nd March to 3rd April neither will the Pataratu thermal power plant run nor will the wheels of Bokaro Steel plant revolve. Not a single speck of forest resource or mineral resource will be allowed to go to any establishment. We have taken this battle as the last battle because in this process several rounds of talks were held and scheme were plotted to derail our movement. But now we have reached on this conclusion that the government was considering our battle as our weakness and everytime tried to move us away from our goals. Therefore, now we have decided that following the path of Gandhi will not work because the government does not understand that language. In order to make them hear our voices it is necessary to break the silence and use those means that are being used by the people of Punjab and Kashmir. In the process of agitation if even one of our workers is martyred his sacrifice will not go in vain. Today we have decided to light a lamp for the martyrs in Morabadi ground because we know that the kind of movement we are going to launch will need a lot of motivation from the martyrs. Today we have come here to take a pledge to forget everything for the next fifteen days and work only to make the movement for a separate state a success. For fifteen days, leaders and workers should forget what tyranny was committed by whom. Which official was suspended or who did police lock up in the process. After the agitation we shall look into what had happened with whom and what needs to be done about that.

Date 22nd October 1999 Place: Ranchi

Only Jharkhandis will run Jharkhand

The bill for the formation of Jharkhand had been passed from the Rajya Sabha as well as Lok Sabha. But the formation was scheduled for 15th November on the anniversary of bhagwan Birsa

Munda. At that time, Shibu Soren was a part of the NDA and he was confident that he only would be made the Chief Minister. The difference between JMM and BJP was rising due to the post of the Chief Minister. JMM was also creating pressure. In the process, Shibu Soren organized a huge rally in Morabadi ground in Ranchi on 22nd October 2000 which was called Vijay Maharally. Shibu Soren's stance in that rally was very aggressive. He had said 'Friends, you shall be prepared for a do or die battle on 15th November. As a part of conspiracy, efforts are being made to keep JMM out of power and that will not be tolerated. Right now we only have got the state of Jharkhand and who shall rule, who will be the chief minister is yet to be decided. All of you should come to Ranchi on the anniversary of Bhagwan Birsa Munda and take a look at the chief minister. If he is not as per the will of people of Jharkhand then prepare yourselves for another battle. George Fernandes had given his assurance that once the separate state of Jharkhand is formed, the first Chief Minister will be from JMM only. Now that promise is being broken. An imposed chief minister will not be accepted at any cost. Those who are being troubled for repayment of loans, they won't have to repay the loans. The appointments that are being done from Patna should stop. If the appointments are done, then the young lads of Jharkhand will not let them join services in Jharkhand. If the government of JMM is formed, only then those sons and daughters of Jharkhand who have studied in villages will get the job of teachers.

Jharkhand will be run by Jharkhandis and not outsiders. Now worry how should Jharkhand be governed. We have got a state, it's not some joke. Cultivate crops, rear cattle and rebuild Jharkhand. New Jharkhand should belong to common people, to you and me and not to the factory owners. Alcohol will be prohibited in the new state. Forest department will be abolished. There will be only one DFO and four clerks. People of forest department only have ruined the forests. Forests will belong to us. In five to seven years, trees will be cut and sold. Half the money will be deposited in government treasury and half will go to the villagers. For the post of sepoy, illiterates will be selected who can climb a palm tree three four times, who can shoot hundred arrows from his bow. They only have to catch a thief. No more eligibility is required. Those who are educated, there will many other job opportunities for them. We have gotten Jharkhand by the grace of god and martyrs. Lalu and centre both were trapped; hence they had to give Jhakhand under compulsion. Jharkhand is a fruit of sacrifice by thousands of friends. Now BJP is conspiring. Shibu Soren is not hungry for the post of Chief Minister. He was sent to jail. Now even if he is hanged one lakh times, it will not matter because his penance is complete, a separate state is formed but as long as he is alive he will not let any body be bullish. Officers with crazy minds would mend their ways. They should stop all misdeeds. B.D.O and C.O should not do something crazy. Those who want to stay can stay here those who don't, may leave. Workers should be cautious. If the police inspectors do not listen to you encompass the police station remove the inspector from his chair and sit on his chair. We have seen too much guns and bullets and we are not frightened. In Jharkhand now, the sepoys will not have to do left right while carrying a rifle of 5 kg. Take a bow and arrow which weighs less than half kg and peacefully run the state. Now the alarms will not ring in the police stations but only dugdugi will play. If the D.C and S.P don't listen, surround them and take on spot decisison.

Date 01st August 2004 Place: Jamtara

BJP wanted to kill me inside the jail

Shibu Soren was facing grave charges. Police was looking for him. He had to resign. He was declared absconding. Just before the surrender, he addressed a huge public meeting in Kanchanbera in Jamtara. In that meeting he had said –

I am neither a fugitive nor an absconder but a victim of conspiracy by BJP. After the formation of Jharkhand, NDA government in the state declared to revoke all the cases related to the Jharkhand movement but my case was not brought up on purpose. There is a deep conspiracy by BJP in this. They want to put me in prison and kill me. BJP is very frustrated after their crushing defeat in the Lok Sabha elections. This is why they are planning to start riots before the upcoming legislative assembly elections. BJP people wanted to create a Gujarat here but I did not let that happen. The Chirudih incident had happened a long time ago. That was a movement against the tradesmen and money lenders. When everybody had forgotten about it and had started living together then after 30 years this matter was brought up. I never raised the slogan of insider and outsider. Hindu, Muslim

Sikh and Christian all are one here. In 35 years, I did not let any one fight; But BJP has tried to defame me. I never licked the boots of management, BDO, sub inspectors etc. I always fought against injustice. In this process, many cases were slapped against me. Cases are slapped only against those who fight injustice. I went everywhere and kept the movement going for 35 years. This is why we got Jharkhand today. When I became the coal and mining minister then the coal, asbestos and bauxite mafia was rattled. The entire mafia system is in cahoots with the BJP and looting the mineral resources. The looters of treasure did not like that a Santhal son becomes a minister. Therefore, they conspired to remove me from the chair. Today I am standing here to tell the entire nation that after Jamtara cases against me are being dug out in Giridih, Dhanbad and many other places. I am not hungry for the chair, therefore I have resigned. I am the son of the poor and have given my word to the poor tribal, this is my only fault. As a conspiracy, a 30 year old forgotten matter has been dug out and it has been propagated against me that I am an absconder and killer. Whereas, I never received the court's warrant. Had I been a fugitive, I wouldn't have visited one village after another for 30 years. BJP insulted the Prime Minister and targeted

Sonia Gandhi using this matter. I respect the order of court. Today I am standing in the people's court tomorrow I will appear in the court. But it is not a crime to go to upper court for justice. What does Advani know about poor and poverty? We did not get the state by putting on a long tika and chanting Ram Ram.

Personal Experience

Actually, this is who Guruji is

When Shibu Soren decides something, he does not sit until he does it. He does not differentiate between day or night. My personal experience has also been the same. It was year 2000. The Jharkhand bill was passed but the state was not formed yet. This incident happened between August and November. At that time, I was working in Jamshedpur. Guruji had to go Delhi. First he had to go to Kolkata by Hatia Howrah and from there he had to catch a flight to Delhi. Workers of Jharkhand got the information that Guruji is going to Delhi via Tatanagar. Therefore a huge number of workers and leaders were waiting for him at the station. When the train reached Tatanagar late in the night the workers welcomed him with slogans. A new state was formed.

Excitement of the workers was at its peak. Guruji was accompanied by his wife. Suddenly Guruji asked a leader there 'where have we reached', 'Jamshedpur' he got the reply. Hearing this Guruji ordered 'call Anuj, I need to talk to him.' I was in my office, four – five kilometers away from the station. Suddenly my associate Sanjiv Bharadwaj gets a phone call that Guruji wants to meet Anuj Kumar. Bring him immediately. Sanjiv told me about this. I understood it must be something important that is why Guruji has called me so late in the night. Hurriedly I reached station along with Sanjiv on his bike. The train was standing at the station. Workers were standing at the track. I knew that train did not have a long halt in Tatanagar but the workers of JMM were running the show. How could the train move forward? I was taken to meet Guruji. We talked for seven or eight minutes. I was feeling bad that other passengers were troubled and the train was still not moving. But Guruji was in no mood to hurry. Whatever information he wanted from me, I gave him. When Guruji was satisfied I asked his permission to leave. After that I got down from the train and after that, the workers moved away from the track. This is how Guruji was. Once he decides on something then nothing worries him.

Author, chatting with Shibu Soren and his wife Roopi Soren inside a train coach at Tatanagar station, just a few days after Jharkhand Bill getting passed by the Parliament during the year 2000.

When he cut his own son's ticket

One accusation is always leveled on Guruji that if it comes to his family, he does not listen to anybody. One example sends this accusation to the dustbin. Guruji had cut his own son, Durga Soren's ticket for a member worker of JMM. Nobody will readily believe this incident but it is true. This is an incident of 2004 Lok Saba elections. JMM was in alliance with Congress. Jamshedpur seat was given to JMM. Sunil Mahto was preparing to contest from that seat for a long time. Champai Soren, Ramdas Soren, Mohan Karmkar, Sunil Mahto, Vidyut Mahto (total 5 – people used to call them pandav) had built a team. Dulal Bhuiyan was not a part of that. Candidatures were not yet announced. Still, it was considered that Sunil Mahto will contest that seat. In the mean time a program was organized in Ghatshila and Guruji made an announcement that Durga Babu will be the candidate from Jamshedpur. It was a blow for the team of Pandavas.

At around 11 in the night, I received a call from my associate Rintu. He asked "Brother, can you come to Mango? Please come. Something wrong has happened. It has been decided to give the ticket to Durga Soren. Everybody is upset." I said 'It is Guruji's party. He will decide. He can give the ticket to whoever he wants. What do I have to do with that? What will I achieve by going there? Anyway, if Guruji has decided, who has the guts to change his descision?' Rintu kept persuading me "You just come. Talk to Guruji just once. Only you can tell him the truth."

I reached Mango. He was there to attend a wedding ceremony. Hundreds of cars were waiting outside. Johar Guruji, I addressed him and sat there beside him. A few moments later I said to him 'Guruji there is something I want to talk to you about.' 'Marriage is going on, what is there to talk now?' he said to me. Then I too remained silent. Nobody said anything for an hour. The atmosphere was getting tense. Sunil, Ramdas, Champai, Vidyut and Mohan were sitting behind me.

Suddenly Guruji got up and started to leave. Everybody got up. I too accompanied him. By that time Guruji sat in the backseat of his car. Champai Soren was with him. His body guard Sharma was sitting in the front. I asked 'Where are you going Guruji?'

He replied 'Bokaro.'

I said 'I will also go to Bokaro with you.'

Guruji said 'Now, in the night?' Anyway, the gate opened and I sat in the car. Dozens of cars were behind Guruji's car. I muster a lot of courage and asked 'Guruji, have you finalized ticket for Jamshedpur?' he said 'Yes, its settled, Durga Babu will contest from there.' I said 'Here the social equatioin is against Durga Babu, you will lose this seat.' I told him 'you are the party president, I am neither a worker nor a member of your party. It is not even right for me to meddle in this matter. You shall decide who will contest I am only giving my advice because you have been seeking my advice on various matters in the past as well and you say that Anuj will speak truth to my face. You only have given this right to me.' I kept on speaking 'out of three seats if father son duo contest on two (Dumka and Jamshepur), then it will not send the right message in public. This seat is Kurmi dominated. Therefore, it will be better to field a Kurmi candidate.'

Guruji asked 'who will be better?' I replied 'that you should decide.'

He asked again 'How about Sunil?' I said 'at the moment only he is preparing.' Guruji did not say anything. I said what I had to say. I told Guruji to stop the vehicle. I will get down here.' By that time, we had reached Pardih. Rintu had also come there behind us. I came back to my office. It was late in the night.

After an hour Mohan Karmkar calls me 'Anuj bhai, it seems some miracle has happened, Guruji has called all of us to Ranchi tomorrow.'

Next day a meeting is conducted at Guruji's residence in Ranchi. Dulal Bhiyan recommends the name of Sunil Mahto and Durga Soren seconds it. Within 24 hours, the entire scenario is changed. Sunil Mahto takes the blessings from Guruji, contests elections, wins and becomes an MP. Later the same Sunil Mahto was killed in a naxal attack in Baguria. Only Guruji could take descision of cutting his owns son's ticket and give it to Sunil

Mahto and that is what he did. Such occasions are rare in politics.

Got sent the dead body of a childhood friend to his home

Guruji was sitting in circuit house in Jamshedpur. I was also there. P N Pandey was his secretary at that time. He was also there. Discussion on other subjects was going on. Suddenly P N Pandey gave the phone to Guruji. Somebody was on the line. A voice says something from the other side. Guruji said in a tone of frustration 'Your father has neither met me nor does he call. Where are you?' Upon hearing the reply from the other side, Guruji's face turned white. His tone changed. He said 'when, when, when? You don't worry I will look into it. Son, I am still alive, everything will be alright.' After that he told Pandeyji 'Call Manjoor (Ansari)'. At that time Manjoor was the owner of Irba hospital. Guruji got angry over the phone itself 'what kind of hospital have you opened Manjoor that the patient dies. When the patient is dead how will he pay? You have taken the dead body in your custody, what will you do with it, will you make lemonade from that? He was my professor friend from BIT. Release the body quickly and hand it over to his son.' This order from Guruji was enough. Actually when the son of his professor friend had called, he was not aware that he had died. As soon as he knew about that he forgot everything and started to work for getting his body sent home. Then he said to Pandeyji 'see to it that they face no problems.' Such was Guruji's nature.

Had doused the fire of Domicile

I am reffering to an incident here. The atmosphere that day was such that if Guruji had not taken a soft posture on that day, the entire Jharkhand would have burnt. Although violence did happen; but one statement from Guruji brought the situation under control. Guruji had risen above party and vote bank politics to issue that statement. In that instant, his supporters might have thought that how did this happen; but overall his image got better. The message that got sent out was that Guruji has called back the bandh for the entire state and has asked his workers to stay away from violence.

The entire story is as follows: A Jharkhand Bandh was called on 20th July 2002 in support of domicile. On that day violent clashes had erupted between the supporrtes and opposers of the bandh in various parts of the state. Bandh supporters had come out on streets armed with traditional weapons. Police also had to fire a few rounds. Many people were injured. Jharkhand was burning. It seemed that now Jharkhand is trapped in a civil war. The state was divided between pro domicile and anti domicile groups. Political parties were left far behind. The only thing which mattered was if one was pro domicile or anti domicile. No leader from any party had the guts to speak clearly on the issue.

On that day, Shibu Soren was in Delhi. He was regularly getting information regarding the situation in Jharkhand. Many associates had given him reports that were blown out of proportion. Guruji was very angry. That night I had a long conversation with him. He was very worried for the situation of Jharkhand. His pain was visible. The violence that was happening was troubling him. He did not want people to fight, beat or kill each other in the name of domicile. He wanted the people of Jharkhand to get third and fourth grade jobs, but he was against any kind of violence to achieve this. On that day I had requested Guruji to check all the information that he was getting. Only then he should issue any statement. A statement from Guruji meant a lot, it was the final call. I gave him all the information over telephone and made a special request to him to issue a statement to calm Jharkhand. He had agreed. The statement he issued that day (although over telephone) had helped a lot in bringing the situation under control.

It was not an easy job to ready Guruji for a statement. When I had started talking, Guruji was very angry and had said Bandh has been called and it will happen. It occurred in my mind that if any wrong message goes out then situation will go out of control. I tried to calm him down and said to him that he was the guardian of Jharkhand, of both pro and anti domicle. The situation went out of control due to a decision taken by the government. In the coming days he too will have to govern the state. Therefore issue a statement to calm down the situation in Jharkhand. Guruji had understood this. He calmed down and said 'what can I do from here?'. Finally he gave a statement which is below, the excerpts from the conversation I had with Guruji on 20th July 2002:

(This report was published in the Jamshedpur edition of Prabhat Khabar on 21st July 2002).

This government will burn the state and take it to the ashes. It has created such an atmosphere that people have come out on streets against each other. Domicile supporters and opponents should stop fighting against each other. Enough is enough. Live in Jharkhand with a sense of brotherhood. People should understand the motive of the Marandi government. It is frustrated after the defeat in Dumka elections and taking its revenge. People have also fallen in their trap and come out on streets shouting domicile domicile and are ready to kill each other. Marandi government has brought out this ghost of domicile and people are running after it. There are no jobs but they are going crazy about the status of domicile. Marandi government understands the people's fears and insecurities. Now people are not talking about other immediate issues but running after domicile. Remove this Marandi government immediately. If we are late, the remaining Jharkhand will also be lost. People will kill each other. The divide between insider and outsider will widen. It is always alleged that JMM causes quarrels among people. Now everybody can see who is actually behind all this. Be it panchayat elections, reservation or domicile. Had JMM been in power we would have talked about jobs, gave employment and not forced people to fight among themselves in order to rule. The kind of decisions Marandi government is taking it seems that they are cutting off the heads of the same people who have put him on the throne, so go and vote for BJP again. When you have made their government be ready to face the consequences. This government is making a fool out of tribals and natives. Nobody will get anything. Both should understand this and sit together to resolve the matter. If the elders of the house sit together and address the issue then such a situation can be avoided easily. It is true that those whose ancestors are named in the last survey will get the jobs and they should as well. But it does not mean that others won't get a job. There is no scarcity of jobs in Jharkhand. If the policies are framed in correct manner then there will be no complaints about jobs. A separate state has been formed. Tribal and natives of the rigion have been ignored for centuries. They have the first claim. If these people get priority in third and fourth grade jobs then what is the objection for? Those who have come from outside, earning their livelihood here, who is chasing them out? Nobody can chase them out. Many non tribals have also sacrificed for Jharkhand. Their ancestors should also be respected. As far as jobs are concerned, first tribals and natives should get some extra benefit. After that as soon as new jobs are created, everyone should be included. Only a few create ruckus. Now see what happened today, the question about domicile was brought by the Marandi government and the opponents burnt the flags of JMM, ransacked its office and pelted stones on Vidyut babu (Vidyut Mahto, who later became an MP from Jamshedpur). All these are conspiracies to incite the Jharkhand Mukti Morcha. JMM wants to take everyone along in the process of development of the state. But if its workers and leaders are attacked, how will JMM sit silent? All these are being done by astute politicians who are sitting in Ranchi and doing all this so that JMM takes some extreme step and entire blame could be shifted on JMM. This is the reason that inspite of all these incitement JMM workers have kept a cool head till now. Everyone living in Jharkhand is a Jharkhandi and everyone will be taken care of but first you should remove this government. If the government of JMM is formed then none of these problems will exist. If people who have lived together for so long will kill each other, if peace is disrupted than what will become of Jharkhand. Did we take Jharkhand for this day?

When this statement by Guruji was published in newspapers next day, people were visibly angry that the bandh was called off, but gradually everything returned to normal. Had Guruji not issued a statement on that day, the situation was bound to go out of control. Only his secretary P N Pandey was aware of this conversation between me and Guruji. I too did not want to tell anyone about this but Pandeyji himself made this information public in a program in Jharkhand that was organized one year later.

Arranged for the Education of a Specially-abled Child

In 2004–05. Jharkhand Mukti Morcha had arranged a meeting in Manoharpur. In order to participate in it, Guruji first went to Jamshedpur. There I went to meet him at the station. He told Dulal Bhuiyan 'Anuj will also come with us to Manoharpur. Arrange for one more ticket. We will talk on the way.' I had no idea that I will have to go to Manoharpur. Anyway, I accompanied him to Manoharpur. The meeting was held. A young boy 13 – 14 years, Gulshan Lohar had also come to that meeting. He had no hands. Guruji called him on stage and put an envelop in his pocket. He also announced that he will take all the responsibilities of his education. After 15 years I tried to take note of whereabouts of the boy. Then I came to know that Guruji had helped him get a B.Ed certificate.

Guruji bearing the entire cost of education for a specially-abled child

Today he has become a teacher (non government). Gulshan can operate a laptop using his legs. He told me that Guruji changed his life. Had he not gotten the support, he would not have been able to stand on his legs today.

List of References

- K S Singh, Tribal movement in India, Manohar 2015.
- S P Sinha, Conflict and tension in tribal society, concept publishing company, New Delhi, 1993.
- Shailendra Mahto, 'Jharkhand ki Samargatha', Danish Books, Delhi, Patna Nagpur, 2015.
- Balbir Dutt, 'Kahani Jharkhand Andolan ki', Crown Publications, 2005.
- Binod Kumar, 'Samar shesh hai', Prakashan Sansthan, New Delhi, 1999.
- Harivansh, 'Jharkhand Disum Muktigatha aur Srijan ke Sapne', Rajkamal Publications, New Delhi, 2002.
- Louis Tillin, 'Remaping India, Oxford University Press', New Delhi, 2013.

- Veer Bharat Talwar, 'Jharkhand Andolan ke Dastavez', Navarun, Ghaziabad, 2016.
- Anuj Kumar Sinha, 'Jharkhand Andolan ka Dastavez, Shoshan Sangharsh aur Shahadat, Prabhat Prakashan, New Delhi, 2012.
- Ajit Rai, 'Fakhra hoga tumhe ki tumne A K Rai ko dekha', Shahar publications, Jharkhand, 2011.
- Dr B Virottam, 'Jharkhand: itihas aur Sanskriti', Bihar Hindi Granth Academy, Patna, 2001.
- Veer Bharat Talwar, 'Jharkhand ke adivasiyon ke bich, ek activist ke notes', Bharatiya Gyanpith, 2012
- A R Desai, 'Repression and Resistance in India', Bombay Popular Publications, 1990.
- 'Shaal Patra', (monthly magazine, Editor: Manmohan Pathak and Veer Bharat Talwar), Dhanbad, 1978.
- 'Jharkhand Varta', (monthly magazine, Editor: Veer Bharat Talwar), 1978.
- 'Nirmal Smriti: Shaheed Nirmal Memorial committee', Jamshedpur, 1987.
- Mukutdhari Singh, 'Swatantrya Sangram: Bhooli Bisri kadiyan', (part 2), Samta Publication, Patna 1978.

- 'Amrit Bazar Patrika', (English daily, Jamshedpur)
- 'Jharkhand Sandesh', (Hindi magazine, Dhanbad)
- 'Dharmyug, Adivasi Asantosh Special Edition', (Hindi weekly, 30th August, 1981) Times of India Publication.
- 'Navbharat Times', Hindi daily, Patna.
- Times of India (Mumbai).
- 'Prabhat Khabar', (Hindi daily), Neutral Publishing House Limited, Ranchi.
- 'Dinmaan', (Hindi weekly), Times of India Publication, 1976, 1978, 1980.
- 'Ravivar' (Hindi weekly), Anand Bazar Patrika Group.
- 'Indian Nation', (English daily), Patna.
- 'Searchlight', (English daily), Patna.
- 'Ranchi Express', (Hindi daily), Ranchi.